AWESOME PURPOSE

Dedication

This book is dedicated to all those – past, present and future – who had, have or will have an awesome purpose, and have the persistence to see it through to completion.

AWESOME PURPOSE

Nigel MacLennan

Gower

Published by
Gower Publishing Limited
Gower House
Croft Road
Aldershot
Hampshire GU11 3HR
England

Gower
Old Post Road
Brookfield
Vermont 05036
USA

Nigel MacLennan has asserted his right under the Copyright, Designs and Patents Act 1988 to be identified as the author of this work.

British Library Cataloguing in Publication Data
MacLennan, Nigel, 1961–
Awesome purpose
1. Organizational change   2. Corporate culture   3. Achievement motivation   4. Employee motivation
I. Title
658.4'012

ISBN 0566 08040 0

Library of Congress Cataloging-in-Publication Data

MacLennan, Nigel, 1961–
Awesome purpose / Nigel MacLennan.
p. cm.
Includes bibliographical references and index.
ISBN 0–566–08040–0
1. Corporate culture   I. Title.
HD58.7.M322   1998
658.4'062–dc21   98–19795
                                                                                          CIP

Phototypeset in Century Old Style by Intype London Ltd
and printed in Great Britain at the
University Press, Cambridge

Contents

Preface

What motivates the kind of super-achievement that top companies seem able to inspire regularly? An **awesome purpose**!

If you went to the NASA of 1965 and asked what their awesome purpose was, what do you think they would tell you?

When Kennedy announced to America and the world that the country would put a man on the moon and return him safely to earth, he unleashed the most awesome purpose in history.

When Winston Churchill announced that Britain was defending democracy and would free Europe, what happened?

When Steve Jobs announced that Apple was going to make computers usable by all, what happened?

When Henry Ford announced that he was going to make cars accessible to all, what happened?

Each of these people unleashed an awesome purpose.

Compare that to what goes on in most organisations. 'Keep good income tax records.' 'Have every member of staff able to use a lathe *and* a milling machine.' 'Increase profits by two per cent.' Can you feel your spine tingling? I thought not! It just does not inspire, does it? If you want superior performance, you must provide a superior cause. Provide a strong enough 'why', and the 'how' will fall into place.

Is this book for you? It is if you want to:

- Be able to define culture.
- Learn why some cultures are perfectly aligned.
- Learn why some cultures in organisations with fewer resources than you have consistently produce much better results.
- Learn how to identify your company culture.
- Understand how culture influences decisions in organisations.
- Identify where you can see your culture in action.
- Pinpoint the link between culture and behaviour.
- Learn how culture is created, spread and changed.
- Demystify culture and strategy for yourself and all your staff.
- Specify the most common confusions in culture and cultural communication.

- Provide a common cultural language that will enable your staff to communicate on the subject of culture.
- Acquire a range of tools for effective culture change.
- Understand the circumstances in which the culture-change tools can be used.
- Know when the best toolbox in the world will be useless.
- Learn what are the 'mutables' and 'immutables' in culture change.
- Identify the most common implementation problems.
- Overcome the most common implementation problems.
- Learn why most culture-change programmes fail.
- Discover what absolutely *must* be in your action plan for culture change.
- Identify the most important elements in effective culture change.
- Establish the current benchmarks and best practice in culture alignment.
- Look at some awesome examples of culture changes/alignments/creations.
- Learn how the CAM, 9R and 6P models work together to achieve culture change.

Awesome Purpose is a 'how to' guide for changing, aligning and unleashing the power in organisational cultures. For the first time, organisations will have a coherent model and framework for culture change. In so doing, *Awesome Purpose* rectifies a significant omission in this field: there is no coherent and integrated framework/model around which to create/align/change a culture. Most, if not all, previous texts provide only a series of tips supported with interesting anecdotes. Great for entertaining after-dinner speeches, but pretty useless when it comes to the serious business of aligning or changing your culture. *Awesome Purpose* will give you that all-embracing business framework which you knew should exist, but were never taught about in business school.

Awesome Purpose and the models contained therein (the Corporate Alignment Model, the 9R Model and the 6P Model) will provide a cradle-to-grave understanding of how to manage culture and its elements. You will be provided with a basis for establishing a shared and agreed understanding of the elements of culture – the first step to effective cultural alignment/creation/change. You will learn about a vehicle which will communicate all elements of a culture to all those affected by that culture. You will discover a mechanism which gives all your staff the guidelines they need to make the decisions they have to make to achieve what the organisation is trying to achieve.

The influence of such commonly misunderstood concepts as 'strategy', 'mission', 'values' and 'operating principles' on the culture of an organisation is spelled out clearly. The role of these concepts within the models will be demonstrated. The CAM demonstrates the relationship between all the elements at work in a culture, and focuses on successful change at the corporate level. The 9R Model is the sequence of events necessary to change or align a culture. The 6P Model is concerned with the factors which have to be considered to implement the CAM and the 9R Model.

Awesome Purpose is a multi-disciplinary work drawing (invisibly) on anthropology, sociology, psychology, leadership studies, organisational behaviour, political science and several other disciplines. The concepts brought together are 'translated' into business paradigms and terminology, but not too much so. As you will see from a brief examination of any of my previous books, they are largely jargon-free.

To achieve anything of substance, you must provide great goals. If you want to see awesome performance from your company, if you want to see a spine-tingling level of alignment amongst your staff, you must provide them with a spine-tingling purpose. If you want awesome performance, you must provide awesome purpose. *Awesome Purpose* will show you how.

Anyone wishing to contact the author can do so by writing to:

Nigel MacLennan
1733 Coventry Road
South Yardley
Birmingham
B26 1DT
UK

Acknowledgements

To a group of people without whom this book and all my previous books would not exist, I offer my sincere thanks, specifically to David J. Newton, whose enormous illustrating talents have consistently turned my matchstick sketches into the professional cartoons which you see before you. Thank you, David. To Sarah Allen, whose editing and English language skills are responsible for making each book easy to read and easy to follow. Thank you, Sarah. To Solveig Gardner Servian and her editing team at Gower for taking such care of my babies. Thank you, Solveig. To Malcolm Stern, whose faith in me was responsible for starting my publishing career. Thank you, Malcolm. To Chris Simpson for offering so many useful ideas for improving this book. Thank you, Chris.

To the companies and organisations with whom I am fortunate enough to work, thank you for the opportunity to help and the forum in which to develop. Thanking each member of staff by name would be inappropriate (but I hope when you see the sections in the book that you recognise from our work together, you will know that that is my acknowledgement to you).

To the thousands of delegates at my seminars and conferences, although I rarely get to know your names and cannot thank you personally, a collective thank you. Thank you for your questions: they tell me how to structure the books, what is of greatest concern to you, what to put in, and just as importantly, what to leave out.

To Patricia MacLennan, my mother, who taught me all the things in life worth knowing; thanks for one thing in particular – teaching me the art of persistence, for without that, this and the other books would not exist.

Part I
Culture

Part I seeks to give you a sufficient depth and breadth of understanding of culture to equip you for the culture-change journey on which you are, presumably, about to embark.

1 Understanding culture

CHAPTER OVERVIEW

- The power of culture
- The need for a common language
- What is culture?
- Defining culture
- The workings of culture: What are memes?
  - Levels of memes
  - How powerful are memes?
  - How far will people go to defend memes?
  - Memetic selection
  - The strongest memes survive
  - Do the strongest memes match reality?
- Cultural protection

THE POWER OF CULTURE

Culture is a very powerful force. When all the members of a culture are aligned, pointing in the same direction and seeking to attain the same ends, it is truly awesome. Most of the greatest human achievements – politically, socially, commercially and technically – have occurred under those circumstances. A well-aligned organisation will always outperform a non-aligned or partially aligned organisation.

To achieve that level of alignment in most settings requires a great understanding of culture and its mode of reproduction. This part of *Awesome Purpose* is designed to give you that understanding.

If culture were not a powerful force, why would oppressive governments since society began have tried to censor incoming information? Why did Stalin try to stop information about the values and culture of the West getting into the Soviet Union? Today, why do some governments prevent (or try to) the use of satellites or the Internet? Because when culture starts to move and change, it is an irresistible force.

So what is the smart thing to do? Learn about culture, learn how it works,

3

An aligned culture

learn what forces shape it, learn what forces change it, learn how to harness it, learn how to unleash its power in a specified direction. *Awesome Purpose* is about harnessing the power of culture, about aligning your culture to harness the combined power of your staff.

THE NEED FOR A COMMON LANGUAGE

Indulge me here. Try an experiment. Leave your office and ask the first twenty people you come across as you do a circuit of the building to define 'strategy'. Go on, try it. When you come back, do you think you will be able to say you have twenty identical definitions? Or do you think you will have twenty different versions, with one or two overlapping each other?

OK, indulge me again. Go out and ask a different twenty people what a 'mission statement' is and how you would recognise an effective one. While you are out, ask another twenty people what the company culture is, and how they define 'culture'. Ask another twenty what a good 'vision statement' looks like. Ask another twenty for the difference between 'operating principles' and 'values'.

Unless you are in one of the companies in this book (or one as culturally well-aligned) the chances are you will have discovered that not only do most people not know what your company culture is (most none the less claim to), but that there are as many definitions of each of the key business terms as there are people in the company.

If people try to communicate when speaking a different language, what happens? Not a lot. When people in a company have different definitions of key business terms and they seek to have a discussion about the future of the business, what happens? Not a lot. Long, protracted discussions that seem to go nowhere and are based on quicksand are normal in such companies.

Clearly, if there is to be any hope of aligning a company culture, everyone must share the same definitions of the key business terms. It does not really matter what those definitions are; what matters is that everyone shares them.

Getting agreement on your terms and getting everyone up to speed on the elements of culture are essential if you are going to align your culture. If there is no shared understanding of culture, there will be no shared culture.

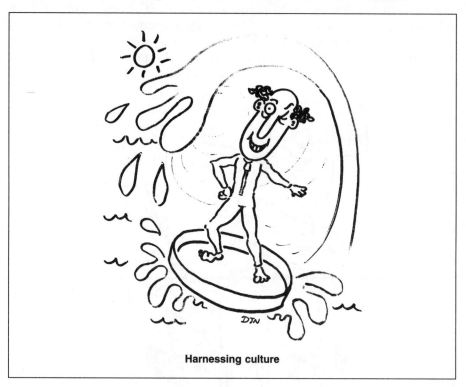

Harnessing culture

One of the central objectives of *Awesome Purpose* is to provide a shared definition of culture, a coherent framework and a common language.

What should that shared definition of culture be? How should you define the key business terms? You could agree your own definitions, or if you are disinclined to spend a considerable time re-inventing the wheel, you could use the definitions here. Again, it matters not what your shared definitions are. What matters is that you have them.

WHAT IS CULTURE?

Where can culture be witnessed? Where does it cease to be an invisible, abstract concept? Every time a decision is made, it reveals your culture in big neon lights. Every structure broadcasts what is valued in the company. All policies say 'this is valued' and 'that is not'. Each and every customer interface situation screams to the customer what your company is, what it values and where it is going. Every tiny detail of your reward systems tells each and every member of staff which behaviours will be valued and which will be ignored or penalised. All your recruitment decisions are a loud-hailer announcement to your existing staff, as are all the people who applied for each post who were not given it. Every time you promote someone, you say to everyone else: 'This is what we

The need to speak the same language

value in this organisation.' Every time you dismiss someone, you address an invisible AGM and say: 'We consider this so unacceptable that we are prepared to dismiss for it.' Every supplier you use and every supplier you reject broadcasts what you are and what your culture is to many of those they come into contact with. Every single thing that goes on in your company reveals your culture. Nothing, absolutely *nothing* can be done which does not either reveal your culture or send signals to others about it.

DEFINING CULTURE

Culture is very difficult to define. Do not take my word: before reading further, try to define it yourself.

Exercise: Define culture.

Stop! Please try to define culture yourself. Try to write down a definition that you would be prepared to stand up and defend. Unless you do that and find out for yourself how difficult a concept it is to pin down, you won't be in a position to appreciate how much difficulty your staff will have with the idea.

Is culture the collective psychological environment? Is it 'the collection of things that people in any defined group do, think, make and say; all their ideas, methods, rituals, artefacts, laws and so on'. That is too long and clumsy a definition. Let's try something shorter: 'a shared set of values which tend to be self-perpetuating'. That does not really work either. Culture is more that just values, it also includes methods, systems, know-how. What we need is some term that includes all of these things. The term is *memes*.

Exercise: Do you know of any other word that describes all the elements just mentioned?

THE WORKINGS OF CULTURE: WHAT ARE MEMES?

Culture is the self-perpetuating collection of memes shared by any group of people.

The concept of memes is not new. It has been around in the social sciences for some time. But what *are* memes? That is best illustrated by an analogy which compares software and hardware to our mental and physical selves. Our genes are the hardware, and our memes are the software. Our genes are expressed as our bodies, our memes are expressed as our behaviour, and all its consequences.

Memes are the beliefs, values, knowledge, know-how, methods, procedures, indeed any discernible unit of information which can be different in one culture from that in another.

Here are some examples. All cultures have some kind of religion, so there must be a meme or a meta-meme for religion. Each culture has laws, so there is a meme for law. Each culture has rites of passage, so there is a meme for that. Each culture has developed its own technologies and methodologies for doing the things all human beings have to do to survive in a collective environment – food-growing, gathering and distribution – so there will be memes for those things.

A meme is a unit of information in a person's head that they believe enables them to function effectively in some context.

Memes and values are like magnetic forces: in themselves they are invisible, but their effect can be seen. Does the meme 'conservation of energy' exist? Human mastery of physics looked very different before its emergence than after it was discovered and spread by Newton. After the publication of Newton's *Principia,* did the world not gradually adopt a more rigorous form of science than the Greek memes gave us? Is 'science' not the most successful meme ever? Does the meme 'justice' exist? The existence of a legal system in every country in the world certainly indicates that. Does the meme 'freedom' exist? People all over the world are and have been prepared to lay down their lives for it. For what were the hundreds of young people murdered in Tienanmin Square peacefully protesting?

Exercise: What memes were behind the American Civil Rights Movement? What memes were fought for in apartheid South Africa? What memes were confronting each other in the Vietnam War?

LEVELS OF MEMES

We all hold several different levels of memes:

- universal memes – shared by all human beings
- meta-memes – a meme for 'religion', 'relationship' memes, a meme for 'organisation', etc.
- supra-regional memes
- geographic region memes
- national memes
- national regional memes
- local memes
- family memes
- individual memes

Usually, we are unaware of them. Some are so pervasive as to be invisible (universal memes). Others (such as national memes) we are only aware of when we see other countries behaving in ways we consider unacceptable (such as chopping off bits of people who commit offences). Usually, we make reference to our memes when we make decisions, and consequently become fully or partly aware of them. 'Aware' need not necessarily mean that we can articulate them. Few people or organisations are fully able to articulate their core memes. Those who can have enormous advantages over those who cannot. (Much more on this later.)

Exercise: What memes are prevalent in your organisation? In your geographical region? In your country? (Becoming aware that you can't yet answer these questions is the point of this exercise.)

Some readers may have realised that there is bound to be a huge connection between genes and memes. We're going to ignore the interplay and interface

9

between memes and genes for the purposes of this subject. It is, after all, a book on organisational alignment, not a social sciences treatise.

HOW POWERFUL ARE MEMES?

People would not be prepared to go to such lengths to spread and protect memes unless there was some enormous advantage in doing so. To give you an idea of how powerful values, memes and culture are, and why they are worth managing, we are going to tiptoe through some of the most striking events and the greatest civilisations in history.

HOW FAR WILL PEOPLE GO TO DEFEND MEMES?

Memes and the need to hold them are so strong that throughout the ages people have been prepared to go to extraordinary lengths. To what lengths? People have been prepared to kill or die to protect their memes. Yes, people will go even to the point of death, even to the point where they will allow their children to die or allow them to grow up without one or both parents. Do you think I go too far? Do you remember this from the Cold War years: 'We would rather be dead than red?'

Exercise: What memes are you prepared to stand up for? What memes have you previously made a stance for?

People need so much for others to share their memes that they will kill those who do not. Religions of all sorts throughout history have faced people with the choice: believe or die. To the shame of Western societies, their dominant religion, Christianity, has been responsible for incredible atrocities in attempts to 'persuade' others to believe. Do you still think I go to far?

Perhaps you think the Spanish Inquisition was just a short-lived fashion for S&M practices? Seriously though, blasphemy was, until surprisingly recently, punishable by death in most 'Christian' countries. In fact, my understanding of UK law is that treason and blasphemy are the only two things for which the death penalty is still in force. Even today, Islamic law states that the death penalty is justified for those who renounce Islam and turn to other religions.

These are expressions of memes at societal level. Surely people do not go to such lengths on a personal level? I'm afraid so. In China there are an estimated 49 million missing women. Why? How? One known cause is infanticide. It is widely reported amongst women who consider themselves 'unlucky' enough to have had a baby girl. The prevalent meme is that male babies are preferred. The same reports have come out of Asia and Africa with similar alarming numbers; 60 million missing women. Can you imagine what powerful forces we are talking about here that could drive a mother to kill her baby girl (or allow her to be killed) soon after birth? That is the power of memes.

Exercise: If you are still not convinced that memes are defended to the death, perhaps you can answer this question. Why do countries engage in ethnic cleansing?

They are driving out that which they consider to be a memetic threat. Ethnic cleansing – perhaps we should call it 'memetic cleansing' – is not new, and it is not limited to barbaric peoples. It has been practised by virtually every country in the world at some time, from the USA (Native American Indians were the victims), Russia, China, Serbia, Indonesia, Germany, England, Cambodia ... We should stop there, otherwise this will turn into an extremely long list. Such is the passion with which people will defend their memes that they are prepared to slaughter millions, and even die themselves.

Is that the kind of force you want to harness for commercial ends? Yes – but I hope we agree you will be using it for good ends, and not in some grotesque attempt to outdo Stalin or Pol Pot!

MEMETIC SELECTION

The nineteenth and twentieth centuries have been a battleground between two great memes: democracy and state control – or as we in the West would put it, freedom and tyranny. As you know, democracy is winning, but still only 40 per cent of the world's population live in freedom at the time of writing.

THE STRONGEST MEMES SURVIVE

Some basic and very old and successful memes that were widely adopted are still in use today: shelter, food storage, water storage, collective hunting, fire, cutting edges. Some slightly more sophisticated memes which conveyed the same advantages are lever, wheel, wedge, axle, pulley and screw. Early humans who adopted those memes increased their chances of survival and procreation over those who did not. Your commercial ancestors may have led the field if they were amongst those who adopted the new memes of their day: irrigation and fertilisation. But as new and more effective memes evolved, if they were amongst those who once led but failed to change, they were left behind. So it is today. Fail to adopt the new memes, and you succeed in destroying your organisation. You knew that, and that is why you are reading this book – to learn about the latest memes for aligning cultures.

A strong meme is one which is believed to provide an advantage to its holders. 'Advantage' can be technological, methodological or social. For instance, a meme which provides a society with greater social cohesion than its competitors lends that society a superiority over others. That is one of the many reasons democracy is the most successful system of communal living ever devised: it involves all its people, and thus creates greater social cohesion.

Exercise: What operating methods (one category of memes) does your company hold that give you advantages in your marketplace?

DO THE STRONGEST MEMES MATCH REALITY?

A strong meme need not match the reality of the world. But if it does not, then a culture holds that meme at its peril. The political, social, technical and commercial environment will select the strongest memes. The strongest memes in the long term are those in tune with the real world and those which are most widely and genuinely held.

Memes which work well in one culture (remember that culture is the collection of memes shared by any group of people) may not work well in another. There is a certain degree of intra-memetic selection. For instance, the concept of the city state worked well in Greece, but when Alexander the Great tried to impose it on his conquered lands, the idea did not take. Their memes were simply incompatible with the 'city state' meme.

Exercise: When you last moved company, did you try to introduce some ideas from your old company to the new one? What percentage of those ideas (memes) were accepted and adopted? Why do you think the percentage was so low?

The great thinker Democritus (*c*460–*c*370 BC) postulated what later became known as 'atomic theory'. That notion was rejected by his peers, and the Aristotelian view was adopted and prevailed for 2 000 years in Western societies. Once selected, for whatever reason, memes will then influence the political, social, technical and commercial environment. The Aristotelian view blocked the advance of physics. It was only when it started to decline as a widely held meme that physics advanced. Since then, technological progress has been accelerating at a faster and faster rate. It makes you wonder: had Democritus's view prevailed, what technologically advanced world would we now inhabit? If the first major physical advances had happened over 2 000 years ago, what kind of world would we now have?

CULTURAL PROTECTION

Usually, a culture is a holistic entity. All parts are closely inter-related, yet their relationship is slowly but constantly changing and evolving. Because culture is a whole, it is subject to changes in part having knock-on effects on all others. That is one reason people resist culture change so much: they instinctively know that one small change can totally upset the order that they have finally been able to understand and exploit.

The protection of a flawed culture against the (threatening) inclusion of effective memes is seen repeatedly throughout history, and usually involves unpleasant behaviour, to say the least. Such is the motivation to maintain the status quo that intelligent, rational and well-educated people will deny irrefutable evidence. Cardinal Bellarmine prosecuted Galileo in 1611 for his 'heretical' suggestion that the earth went round the sun. Why? Because to accept Galileo's evidence (note 'evidence', and not 'hypothesis' – Bellarmine and the others involved had seen the evidence using Galileo's telescope!) would have destroyed the assumptions upon which their culture or memetic code was based. But failure to adopt new memes which can be proven effective weakens a culture more than the adoption of the new meme. As the Christian movement has failed to adopt effective memes which emerged throughout the centuries, it has declined in influence.

Exercise: What effect do you think banning barrier-based contraception in the era of AIDS would have on the influence of any religious movement having such a policy?

In commercial terms, protection of memes is very sensible when there are none better available, but is suicide when new memes emerge which are both more effective and more appealing. Such is the case in the world-wide movement to increase democracy in the workplace. Many organisations are forcefully resisting it despite the overwhelming evidence that it is much more effective than workplace autocracy when adopted. Ironically, the best example I know of industrial democracy (Semco) is in a country not well known for its democratic past: Brazil.

Exercise: Which systems do you currently have set up to protect your organisation's memes?

2 The effects of culture

CHAPTER OVERVIEW

- Memes and culture in the great civilisations
  - Ancient Greece
  - Ancient Egypt and Rome
- New memes
  - The Indus Valley Civilisation
  - China
  - Mesopotamia
  - Aztecs and Incas
- Memetic integrity
  - Early USA
  - The Communist meme
- Culture and behaviour in organisations
  - Memes control the mind and behaviour
  - Human meme pool
- Memetic control
  - Culture and behaviour
- How do people make decisions in organisations?
  - Effective culture
- What is the ideal culture?

MEMES AND CULTURE IN THE GREAT CIVILISATIONS

ANCIENT GREECE

The ancients Greeks were very fond of knowledge. They were the first to organise the systematic collection, testing and dissemination of knowledge. Out of that came the memes we now call 'science' and 'education'. Those memes put the Greeks at the top of the tree for a very long time.

ANCIENT EGYPT AND ROME

Ancient Egyptian society remained unchanged for 3 000 years, from 3100 BC until the Romans came along with more effective memes in 30 BC. One of the memes held in highest esteem (a meta-meme) in the Egyptian culture was 'change is to be avoided and is dangerous'. What was the consequence of that? A 3 000-year-old culture was destroyed in months by an upstart culture with superior memes: long-distance communication methods, road-building techniques, mobile resource management know-how, and possibly most effective of all, the willingness to adopt any meme, method or approach that could be shown to be more effective than their current ones.

The Romans were memetic scavengers, prepared to pick up any useful meme they stumbled across in their conquests. Even their famous road-building meme was learned from the Etruscans. Once adopted, the Romans spread the meme all over Europe.

Exercise: What is the commercial equivalent of the Romans invading and swamping the Egyptians?

NEW MEMES

Bringing in some new memes and dovetailing them in to your existing culture is one sure way to increase your likelihood of commercial strength (sociologists call this 'syncretism'). It is the equivalent of two peoples from separate gene pools mating and producing a third and new gene pool of people who are genetically superior to either of their genetic predecessors. African and Western music were combined to produce Reggae. Like it or loathe it, there is no denying that it has been and continues to be a highly successful new form of music – superior in that it appeals to at least two different cultures.

Exercise: What commercial mergers do you know of that had the same effect as above?

THE INDUS VALLEY CIVILISATION

One powerful meme has ruled the Indian subcontinent for at least 2 000 years, and maybe even for 4 000 years since the Indus Valley civilisation (2000 BC): the 'caste' meme. At birth, one's role, behaviour and social standing are defined by the caste into which one is born. This meme survives and thrives today. Why? Because virtually everyone carries it in their head. Memes do not survive unless people carry them. Memes do not thrive unless they bring some benefit to those who carry them.

CHINA

China first came into existence as the unified state covering the area we now recognise around 221 BC. Many of China's memes are based on the teachings of Confucius (551–479 BC). Four in particular have governed Chinese society for nearly 2 500 years:

1. Government positions and entry into government are based on merit, with merit being determined by learning (meritocracy).
2. Maintain strict control of the economy.
3. All surplus labour is to be used on mass construction projects (that was what built the Great Wall of China in only ten years!).
4. Most knowledge in the hands of the population is dangerous.

Exercise: What memes do you think China will have for the next twenty years, given that they are experimenting with 'one country – two systems'?

MESOPOTAMIA

The 'writing' meme first evolved in Mesopotamia (now southern Iraq) in around 8000 BC. It won't come as any surprise to business managers that it was first used for accounting purposes. Indeed, that was its main use for thousands of years. It was a meme that provided substantial benefits to those who had it. The writing meme has evolved since then, as you might have noticed. It is now so powerful and pervasive that every civilised country in the world starts teaching it to its infants.

AZTECS AND INCAS

These were located in modern-day Mexico and Peru respectively. Two interesting facts:

1. With superior warfare memes, 168 Spanish soldiers were able to defeat the Inca empire of 12 million in three years. The Aztecs similarly fell within a year. Diseases played a large part, but not enough to explain so few defeating so many.
2. Today, 60 per cent of all the world's food is descended from the crops grown by the Aztecs and Incas. Their cultures may have died, but their strongest memes now dominate human eating habits.

In memetic evolution – as in genetic evolution – each meme carries with it something of its predecessors. Our current food memes carry with them much of their memetic predecessors.

Exercise: What is the commercial equivalent of that?

MEMETIC INTEGRITY

Cultures are at risk of collapse if they do not maintain their memetic unity. While the Romans were memetic scavengers, they were also aware that it was necessary to protect their core memes or core values. Cato the Censor was appointed in 184 BC to prevent memes from the conquered Greek culture swamping Roman culture. He failed. The Romans had already adopted the Greek alphabet (you read a variant of it now). Following that were Greek attitudes to the arts and literature, Greek education methods (you were educated according to them), Greek ceramics and metallurgy, and so on. Whether that caused the collapse of the Roman Empire is a matter of debate, but just as with the Incas and Aztecs, the best of the Roman Empire's memes are still with us today. One of many hundred possible examples is Roman law – first written on The Twelve Tablets in 450 BC, it is the basis of most legal systems in the world today.

Exercise: What are the memetic roots of your organisation? When were its values first documented? What were they? Where can you still see their effect today?

EARLY USA

Let's move a little more up to date. What was the evolutionary path of the memes which led to the writing of probably the most influential single non-religious document in history: the US Constitution?

John Locke (1632–1704) published his *Two Treatises of Government* in 1690. He said that government was for the governed, and only legitimate with the consent of the governed. Without consent, revolution was the only right and just thing to do. Thomas Jefferson (1743–1826) had studied Locke's works in detail. He presented the fundamental principles which were a short time later to form the basis of the American Constitution:

1. All men are equal and endowed with certain inalienable rights, life, liberty and the pursuit of happiness.
2. Governments are created by men to protect those rights.
3. Government is legitimate while it protects those rights and has the support of the people.
4. When a government fails to deliver those rights it is the right of the people to change it.

Later, Lincoln uttered the immortal words, 'Government of the people, by the people, for the people', giving a surge to the democratic wave which still ripples around the world today.

Never before in history had the leaders of a nation been so aware of the need to set down in writing the values and principles that would guide that nation from then on. Clear values give awesome power to those sharing them. And look at that culture now: the richest and most powerful nation the world has ever seen. Unlike all previous holders of that crown, the USA has no imperialistic intent, it makes no claims on any other territory. Why? Because one of its central memes (a value, in this instance) is liberty.

Exercise: Name just one of the highest values held by your country.

THE COMMUNIST MEME

Moving more up to date still, let us look at the Communism meme. Why did it fail? It seeks to create a society where all co-operate for the greater good. A sensible objective. Co-operation as a successful meme is dependent on two more fundamental memes: inclusion and assertion. People have a strong need to be included and to be so for what they actually are; almost as strong is the need to assert oneself. People will buy into the co-operation meme if the two more basic memes are expressed (satisfied). Communism failed because it sought to force co-operation without allowing individuals to be included while expressing and asserting themselves.

Exercise: In the UK, during the 1970s, union bullying was reviled by the whole country. Why? What memes do you think were threatened by that behaviour?

CULTURE AND BEHAVIOUR IN ORGANISATIONS

MEMES CONTROL THE MIND AND BEHAVIOUR

Different memes will have a powerful direct effect on thinking and behaviour even when all other circumstances are identical. In many developing countries, living in a brick-built three-bedroom house with a weatherproof roof, central heating, clean, running hot and cold water, a television, video recorder, cooker, fitted kitchen, carpets, furniture, beds and a guaranteed income is considered to be affluence of an amazing order – so much so that such people engage in philanthropic thoughts and behaviour (a classic sign of self-perceived wealth). In a Western democracy, people living in an identical house on a municipal estate receiving a state-provided and guaranteed income (imagine that in a developing country) consider themselves to be in deep poverty and engage in classic self-pitying and victim-type behaviours. The difference? The memes of the societies mentioned are very, very different. One group perceives themselves to be extremely wealthy, and the other poverty-stricken. One group's memes define wealth in the same way as the other's define poverty.

Exercise: If freedom were one of your highest values, how would you perceive being an employee in a huge, autocratic organisation? If order and control were your highest values, how would you perceive working in an anarchic organisation?

HUMAN MEME POOL

If you have done much travelling (I have been privileged to do so through my work), you may have marvelled at the multitude of ways human beings do the same kinds of things. Most of us have furniture, but the variety of ways it is expressed is amazing. We all eat food, but the variety is mouth-watering. When you marvel at the variation between cultures, you marvel at the human meme pool.

The nature and type of children's toys vary with culture. They reflect the memes their parents are seeking to have their children adopt. When kids play with those toys, they are being memetically programmed for that culture. Even the different toys given to girls and boys say a lot about the memes each gender is expected to adopt.

Exercise: Ask a range of your friends what toys they buy for their children, and why? Note the answers to 'Why?': they will reveal the values and other memes held by them.

MEMETIC CONTROL

We are at the beginning of a new age. We are now able to control our genes. Who knows what we will be capable of by the time you and I are old. Awareness of our gene-control knowledge is making us think about controlling other evolved aspects of human living: our memes.

Learning is about successively adopting more effective memes. Your genes only replicate once in a lifetime (your children are only half your genes), but your memes can evolve and replicate many times in your lifetime.

In the last few years there have been no end of articles and books about controlling values and managing cultures and culture changes. We are now aware that we can control our memes. Those who utilise that knowledge in a commercial context can expect to be handsomely rewarded. Those who fail to use it can expect to be left a long way behind. Controlling our memes controls our future. *Awesome Purpose* will give you what you need to harness and direct your organisation's memes and control your future.

Memes influence behaviour, and memes are inferred from behaviour.

Memes have a strong feedback effect on us. First our memes shape us, then we shape our memes, and then they shape us ... Thinking on an international level, let's take 'family' as an example: first we design family structures, then our family structures redesign us. Remember that there are many different

21

forms of family in the world, not only the two by two so common in the West (or should I say, that *was* so common in the West?) – for instance, one wife several husbands, one husband several wives, communal, and so on.

CULTURE AND BEHAVIOUR

What is the connection between culture and behaviour? If you ask yourself some questions, the connection becomes clear. Why do Muslims and Jews not eat pork? What is the connection between behaviour and culture? If someone regularly eats fish on Fridays, what could it tell you about their culture?

Exercise: What do your most prominent behaviours say about your values?

Cultural awareness and sensitivity is essential if you wish to deal successfully with or within any group. Culture is essential for shared human living. It provides a framework for dealing with other people without having to make a huge number of decisions each time you interact. Most of the decisions are already made. Culture therefore provides a strong set of guidelines with which to deal with the wider environment.

All companies have a culture which guides behaviour, whether they acknowledge it or not, whether they have articulated it or not.

Exercise: Looking at the last five things you did at work, how were they influenced by your culture (perhaps in the way they were done or how they were done, or the fact that they were done at all)?

HOW DO PEOPLE MAKE DECISIONS IN ORGANISATIONS?

Quite simply: by reference to the culture. People make decisions against what is usually an invisible and unspoken framework. They make the decisions for which they think they will be rewarded. The way in which they make those decisions is the way they think will bring them rewards. They make decisions by comparing their proposed behaviour against the rewards or penalties they received for previous behaviour. And how are those rewards or penalties dispensed? Ultimately, by the highest-level persons in the organisation referring to their values, or what they believe are the central values of the organisation, in conjunction with what the organisation is seeking to achieve. To the extent that the subordinate's decision is helping towards the organisation's objectives and is in line with its values, the decision or behaviour will be suitable for reward or praise. Naturally, the opposite is also true.

What is the connection between culture and behaviour? In short, culture determines behaviour in conjunction with the targets of the organisation. A well-aligned culture provides guidance for everyone at every level in the organisation.

Exercise: Look at the last five decisions you took at work. What reference did you make to your culture when making those decisions? Imagine a culture diametrically opposed to the one in which you currently work: how would your five decisions turn out in that culture?

EFFECTIVE CULTURE

For a culture to be effective, it must match the vision, mission and strategy of the organisation. A culture with such a match plays like a perfectly tuned piano. One without such a match will make the most expensive caterwauling sounds you can imagine, for a while, before its ultimate demise, before somebody (the marketplace) takes a sledgehammer to it. To throw in another image: an organisation which has its culture failing to match its vision, mission and strategy is like a freight ship sailing with all its anchors down – you may make some progress, but because other ships get to port and back faster, you will be uneconomic for potential customers to use.

WHAT IS THE IDEAL CULTURE?

There is never an 'ideal culture' in the absolute sense the phrase conveys. There can only be an ideal culture for a context, for a time and place. OK, so what would be the ideal culture for our immediate future?

In my opinion, it must be responsive to its environment, flexible in the way it works, change-embracing, and yet highly focused on what it is currently trying to achieve. Amongst its many memes, the effective organisation of the future will increasingly hold flexibility as a value. I believe companies will be judged as much for their ability to change quickly as for their profitability by potential investors. Indeed, I foresee that we will start to develop 'flexibility measures' for that very purpose before long.

Exercise: What kinds of measures do you think would/could assess flexibility and cultural responsiveness?

What are the best values to hold? Those you genuinely hold. You will stick to those more truthfully. It is probably better to find an industry in which the values you hold are rewarded than to try to hold values that you do not really believe just to get the rewards of a lucrative industry.

If you do not hold, for example, flexibility as a value, you are making a bed of nails for yourself by trying to live by it. By all means adopt it as an operating principle, but do not elevate it to the status of value if it is not genuinely that. (We will look at the difference between operating principles and values later.) It is possible to change your beliefs and values, but that is a different subject.

Exercise: What do you think you would do if you were faced with a decision that forced a choice between a value you genuinely held and one you thought was expedient to hold? Would you decide in favour of the former or the latter? If the latter, what signals do you think that would send?

3 Cultural reproduction and management

CHAPTER OVERVIEW

- Cultural evolution
- How is culture reproduced?
  - Symbols in cultural reproduction
  - Imitation in cultural reproduction
  - Experience in cultural reproduction
  - Education in cultural reproduction
- Cultural broadcasting
- Espoused versus actual culture
- Variations in culture
- Managing and aligning cultures
  - Does change lead, or is it followed?
- Summary

CULTURAL EVOLUTION

How do cultures evolve? Largely under the influence of the factors in the environment: neighbouring cultures, the preceding culture, technology, availability of resources, interest groups, persuasive individuals. Like most things in nature, cultures evolve by reproducing. Understanding how culture reproduces is central to understanding how it evolves and how it can be changed.

HOW IS CULTURE REPRODUCED?

It must be learned. Brace yourself for a bit of jargon: the anthropological term is 'enculturation'. The business term is 'induction programme' or 'probationary period'. Culture is learned through four main vehicles:

- symbols

- imitation
- experience
- education

SYMBOLS IN CULTURAL REPRODUCTION

Symbols have been used to convey culture for as long as humans have existed. Indeed, the symbols can often be all that is left of a business or society after it has disappeared. Symbols in corporate life can be an object (a logo, flag, uniform, uniform adornments, company car size, office size, etc.); a pledge or oath of

How cultures reproduce

allegiance (your company slogan, major clauses in your employment contract); a song (national or company anthem); an action (ceremonies, rites of passage, etc.).

Symbols are used to convey memes (values, methods or ideals, etc.). What are the symbols in your organisation? They are highly revealing of the values at work in your culture. How do you get symbols to reveal their memes or values?

1. Identify the symbol.
2. Determine the meaning of the symbol.
3. Identify the specific behaviours, methods or practices it seeks to encourage.
4. Determine what value or ideal is behind the message contained in the symbol (see the section on values, pages 69–83, for assistance in this).

IMITATION IN CULTURAL REPRODUCTION

Much enculturation (induction) is achieved by imitation. Almost everyone in your culture will have learned much of that culture by copying their superiors. This particular means of cultural transmission makes it difficult to determine what value is beneath the imitation: people will copy the behaviours of their superiors without actually thinking what value they are picking up.

Imitation

One company I dealt with recently cross-examined and criticised all proposals if they were from junior managers, but accepted almost unread and praised proposals if they were from other directors. On asking what was going on, I was met with blank stares; no one was aware of the problem. Further pressing revealed: 'That's the way things have always been done here.' Eventually, we discovered that there was an unwritten assumption: 'You don't question senior management.' This company was in trouble. They had lost touch with their customers. Senior managers had isolated themselves, their decisions went unquestioned, unexamined. They were right even when they were wrong. Worse, they were right even when they didn't have enough information to be right or wrong!

Naturally, we would all like to think this was just an isolated incident, but deep down we all suspect this kind of scenario is widespread. Many millions of people are working in corporate cultures created and spread by blindly copying the behaviour of the top team.

Exercise: Over the course of a week, try to spot imitating behaviours. Observe others when in the presence of their superiors, and note the difference in the person's behaviour when their boss is gone. Then turn the spotlight on yourself under the same circumstances.

EXPERIENCE IN CULTURAL REPRODUCTION

Experience teaches us what is not culturally acceptable. If we repeatedly receive negative reactions to some behaviour, we soon learn that it is culturally unacceptable. Conversely, if we receive regular positive reactions to something we are doing, we are being taught what is culturally acceptable, and if we are like the vast majority of other human beings, we will continue with the pleasure-bringing behaviour.

Exercise: Who are you currently praising, and for what? Are they doing more of it? Who are you currently reprimanding, and for what? Are they doing less of it?

EDUCATION IN CULTURAL REPRODUCTION

Induction is largely achieved through education, whether formal or informal, whether by parents, teachers, coaches, peers, subordinates or superiors. In most organisations, the induction (enculturation) programme is started in the interview process, taken further by those leading the induction programme, confirmed by superiors and peers, and periodically updated by trainers and others.

Exercise: Have a look at your induction programme. What percentage of it is cultural information?

CULTURAL BROADCASTING

Every symbol, every behaviour, every decision creates, reveals and perpetuates your culture just as surely as if it were broadcast screaming down the TV tube. Who gets promoted sends huge signals to all in the company about what is valued. If it is turf protection and one-upmanship, then expect more and more of the same. If, on the other hand, the promotee is known for their willingness to help others and solve complex problems in a way that all those involved buy into, then you should expect to see more of that. Be very careful about who you promote. Promote the autocrats, the Machiavellis, the control freaks and you'll soon have an organisation full of them. Of course, if that is what you want then go right ahead – make their day.

Exercise: Think of the last five promotions in your company. If you were to use those to define your culture, how would you describe it?

Xerox promotes, and makes it known that it promotes, its cultural ambassadors, and as a result has a strong, defined and responsive culture.

ESPOUSED VERSUS ACTUAL CULTURE

What do you think people do when an organisation claims to hold one set of values but actually holds another. One multinational client called me in to help them figure out why they could not get their staff or managers to come up with any innovative ideas, and on the rare occasions where they did, everyone was 'too busy' to test them. On closer examination of the culture, and in particular of some recent dismissal decisions, something very revealing turned up. The company espoused innovative values wholeheartedly, but what was actually in place was a 'one strike and you are out' policy – there was zero tolerance of mistakes. Innovation requires risk, and risk inevitably entails making mistakes, but no one wanted to make mistakes for fear of losing their job. Result: no innovation. I am pleased to say that company has now changed its attitude to mistakes, and has already seen considerable innovation. All the bottled-up ideas came flooding out after the senior managers started setting an example and making mistakes.

Exercise: What does your organisation actively encourage on one hand yet make impossible on the other? If the answer is 'nothing', you should learn a little more about your culture: few if any cultures are devoid of contradictions.

VARIATIONS IN CULTURE

Do not assume that it is necessary to have an organisation full of cloned zombies to have an aligned culture. It is not. Only the core values, the central part of the culture, must be uniform. Every other part can vary within wide parameters. Let us illustrate why that is necessary, indeed desirable.

The attitudes and beliefs necessary to be a successful accountant are different from those required to be a successful marketeer. Both groups can hold the same core values, purpose and vision in their minds, but they have different peripheral values which are necessary to function as effective professionals in their fields. We all move in several different cultures and manage to maintain our core personal values. In the group of friends you exercise with, you have your own mini-culture (note the avoidance of the term 'subculture' because of its negative connotations). The same applies to those with whom you share your artistic, literary or musical interests. (There is much more on culture types in the section on recognition; see pages 176–180.)

Exercise: By listing the values of the different cultures you move in, distil those that are common to all the groups. Those are your personal core values.

MANAGING AND ALIGNING CULTURES

Most of us fortunate enough to live in the civilised Western democracies sub-scribe to the values they all share. But each democracy has its own cultural variation. So it is with most companies (not that companies are very democratic: in fact, some make the regimes of Stalin, Mao Tse Tung and Hitler look like training grounds for 'lefty pinko liberals'). There may be many mini-cultures, but there is one larger, all-embracing culture into which everyone buys.

DOES CHANGE LEAD, OR IS IT FOLLOWED?

Whatever the answer, management never produces change. Only leadership can do that. Managers maintain the status quo; leaders create it. Leadership may be no more than the provision of a vehicle to channel a rising cultural momentum, but it is still different from management. Management seeks to contain anything that upsets the status quo. Neither do you have to be in a position of authority to effect massive change, but you can if – and only if – you are in tune with an identified cultural momentum.

Martin Luther King, Ghandi and Nelson Mandela are memorable because they were not in positions of authority when they achieved their amazing successes. They were the vehicles for a huge cultural momentum. They stand out in modern history because they achieved mammoth change without being in authority. If you are not a history student, do you know who abolished slavery in the UK? Do you know who was responsible for introducing a public water supply in the UK? Probably not; but why? Because most types of change take place from the top. It only stands out when it is driven by those not in authority, those who are outsiders. At the cutting edge of change, effective leaders need both. They usually have the objectivity of a detached outsider while having the authority and influence of an insider.

Exercise: Who do you consider to be the most successful leader of change you have ever personally met? Were they as described above? If so, what did they do that gave them their influence as an insider? What did they do that indicated their outsider objectivity?

Change apparently caused by a strong leader or group may not be as it seems. Strong leaders may become so because they see cultural momentum or pent-up frustration resulting from a lack of much-needed change, see the direction in which the force for change is headed, and then provide a conceptual vehicle which the members of a culture seize on and support as though it had been long awaited. Some in the group then proclaim they have some great person in their midst, when, in fact, all they have is someone who read the writing on the wall and read it back to those who wrote it.

In Britain in the latter part of the 1970s there was a huge anti-union feeling. Militant and unreasonable union leaders had repeatedly held the country to ransom, and on several occasions had brought the country to a halt. Every thinking person knew they had to be brought back under control. Mrs Thatcher, then Leader of the Opposition, provided exactly what was wanted.

The Conservative government of the late 1990s, it seemed to the country, was becoming more and more corrupt. Minister after minister was caught engaging in 'self-serving behaviour', MP after MP was caught with their 'nose in the trough'. Lying and being caught lying to parliament was no longer considered a sackable offence for ministers. The entire government saying one thing before an election and doing exactly the opposite within weeks of winning an election became an acceptable way of staying in power. The Conservative Party had become self-serving, arrogant and out of touch with the people. Their only vision was to stay in power for its own sake. There was a huge cultural momentum for a government that had a vision for the country; for a government that wanted to use power to achieve that vision, a government that would keep its promises, that would clean up the standards of public ethics, that would take extremely heavy action against corrupt politicians and officials.

Tony Blair was elected leader of the Labour Party some three years prior to the 1997 General Election. He made promises to his party, and kept them. He laid out a strong and clear vision for his party, and stuck to it until it was achieved. He took heavy action against Labour Party members whose behaviour was less than admirable. Witnessing that, the British people gave him victory at the 1997 General Election by a record majority.

Do those things make Thatcher and Blair great leaders, or do they make them people wise enough to read the writing on the wall? Who knows? Does it matter? They both offered exactly what Britain needed at the time it needed it.

What matters is not whether great leaders cause change or just read the cultural momentum, but that you, as a business leader, must look at the cultural momentum and provide a clear and attractive path to get to some destination point in that direction. As I have already said, you need the objectivity of a detached outsider while having the authority and influence of an insider.

Exercise: The person you thought of for the last exercise: did they ride a cultural momentum wave, or did they start it? How?

SUMMARY

Culture is an extremely powerful force. It exists only when there are shared memes in those who make up the culture. Those memes then influence or even control the behaviour of the members of a culture, they affect the way decisions are taken, and dictate what decisions are taken.

If you understand how culture is reproduced – through imitation, education and so on – you are in a position to change that culture, at least conceptually. In Part II we will move on to looking at the models that will enable you to change and align culture practically.

Part II
The Framework

Part II aims to provide you with a framework with which to understand cultural alignment and change. To do so, several models and intellectual tools are presented.

The Corporate Alignment Model

4

CHAPTER OVERVIEW

- The framework
  - Clearly defined terms
  - Common language
  - The concept of memes is too blunt an instrument
- The context of the CAM
  - Culture-matched change
- Purpose
- Values
- Direction
- Vision
- Mission
- Strategy
- Major objectives
- Tactics
- Objectives
- Operating principles

Culture change cannot be achieved by one person, no matter how talented. Only the constituents of a culture can change that culture. Even a dynamic team of high achievers will struggle. What is needed is a system, a framework. One person or team can create the framework which makes the constituents of a culture wish to change their behaviour.

Can you imagine trying to change or align a culture without a coherent framework for doing so? Probably not; you may even have bought this book to find a suitable framework. Yet thousands of companies and even more consultants all over the world are, as we speak, trying to change or align cultures with no clear framework, with all the likelihood of success of slugs learning to fly.

THE FRAMEWORK

The Corporate Alignment Model (CAM) for the first time gives organisations a coherent model and framework for culture alignment and change: not anecdotes about the small issues in change, the skills needed for or the causes of change (although those peripheral issues will be covered in the 9 Rs), but an all-encompassing, integrated and coherent framework through which you can make any and all reasonable changes in the short term, and with which you can manage your culture in the long term.

CLEARLY DEFINED TERMS

What is the influence of such commonly misunderstood concepts as 'strategy', 'mission', 'values' and 'operating principles' on the culture? What is the difference between 'values' and 'operating principles'? The CAM demonstrates the role of these concepts in aligning and managing a culture. A new model is rarely understandable in the language of the old. For that reason, I will provide clear definitions of all the terms used.

COMMON LANGUAGE

What are the shared and company-wide terms to describe the elements of culture? You probably don't have any. You probably have a wide range of different terms and phrases used to define culture, none of which are shared. The CAM provides a basis for establishing a shared and agreed understanding of the elements of culture – the first step to effective cultural alignment/creation/change.

Do you have a simple and effective way of communicating your culture to those who need to know it? Is it a policy manual? You know how people hate those! Is it a complex set of rules for each department? You know how that disempowers those who need to understand the workings of other departments. The CAM provides a single simple vehicle with which to communicate all the elements of a culture to all those affected by that culture. It provides a mechanism which gives all staff the guidelines they need to make the decisions they have to make in order to achieve what the organisation is trying to achieve.

THE CONCEPT OF MEMES IS TOO BLUNT AN INSTRUMENT

The concept 'memes' helps us to understand culture and its mode of transmission, but it is far too blunt an instrument to use for the purposes of harnessing or aligning culture. It is a catch-all term. It gives a label to the collection of parts that make up culture. To illustrate: you may know that genes (DNA) transmit life, but you need to know what specific genes to transmit in order to breed a champion racehorse. 'Meme' is the general term for a unit of cultural reproduction, but we need to know which specific memes at which level must be in place to create our desired commercial thoroughbred. Descriptions of the different elements become rather clumsy if we start talking about 'operating principle memes' and 'value memes'. For that reason I will from now on only make reference to memes when we are talking about *all* the elements of culture.

THE CONTEXT OF THE CAM

No business-thinking tool can stand on its own; it must be used in conjunction with others. The Cultural Alignment Model is the highest-order tool. All other tools, models, systems, structures must operate within the framework it establishes. But hold on a second: you might say that we had a culture before we thought about using this model. Indeed we did. It too was the highest-level framework into which everything else fitted. The advance is in the fact that now we have a model with highly specific elements to enable us to understand the framework, whereas previously all we had was a vague awareness – we knew there was a culture, we had mission statements, we knew the CEO was instrumental in creating and shaping our culture, but we were not able to articulate the culture and all its elements. Consequently, it couldn't be examined or communicated in any concise form. Now that the elements have been distilled, we have a much more effective way to manage, change or align a culture.

CULTURE-MATCHED CHANGE

For any organisational change to be successful, it must be based in the culture of that organisation. Changes imposed on a culture which are incompatible with that culture will be shaken off immediately. For change to be successful, it must be drawn from and be in tune with the organisational culture. Culture change must be based in and on the culture for which change is sought. That is why the most important part of culture change is to:

1. Understand your culture.
2. Then articulate it in a way everyone can share and use as a basis for communication about the culture.

   No culture cognisance, no culture change. No culture language, no culture change.

Now that the introduction has been completed, let's get down to explaining the elements of the model, one at a time. The diagram below gives an overview of the Corporate Alignment Model.

PURPOSE

PURPOSE DEFINED

Purpose is the thing the organisation will always be doing; it is why the organisation exists.

STATUS IN THE CAM

This, along with values, is 'who you are'.

WHAT DOES PURPOSE DO?

It provides the highest-level focus for an organisation. If all other guidelines have not been able to provide you with a decision, this one should.

PREFERRED FORM OF EXPRESSION

Purpose is expressed as a phrasal verb, for example: 'to improve mental effectiveness'.

Some examples (some are actual, others are inferred from commercial behaviour) include:

- 3M – 'to solve unsolved problems'
- Disney – 'to make people happy'
- MacLennan – 'to improve mental effectiveness'

PURPOSE EXPANDED

Purpose must switch people on. It should give the company and your staff a lifetime and never-ending pursuit. It is that which you will always be doing. A purpose is something that never stops, as distinct from a vision or mission, which have discernible end points. In companies where the purpose is not known, you'll see many platitudes instead, such as 'to optimise return on capital'. Can you imagine inspiring a country to fight for itself 'to protect the cash of those who have invested in our stock market'. Definitely not. Yet tens of thousands of company 'leaders' think exactly that notion expressed in different words will empassion their staff. I think not. What do you think?

Exercise: What is your organisation's purpose? Is it articulated, or assumed? If it is assumed, test the assumption. Go out of your office and ask the first twenty people you meet: 'What is the purpose of our company?' Don't prompt them, just ask the question repeatedly until it is clear that they either don't understand the question or don't know the answer. Both of those outcomes tell you what you want to know.

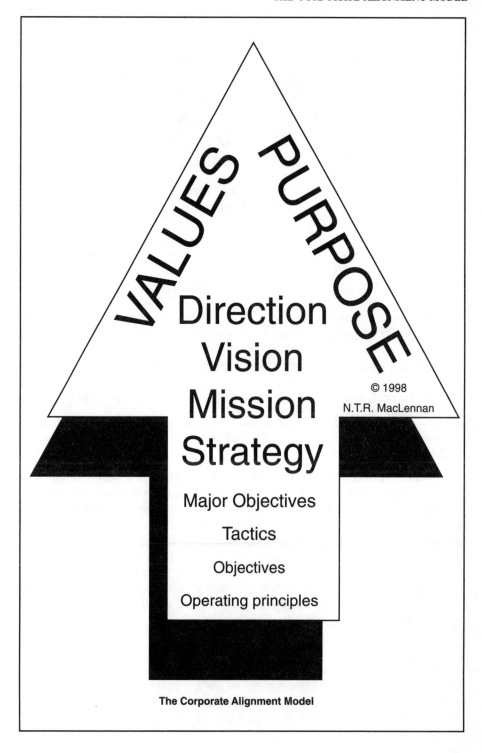

VALUES PURPOSE

Direction
Vision
Mission
Strategy

© 1998
N.T.R. MacLennan

Major Objectives
Tactics
Objectives
Operating principles

The Corporate Alignment Model

1. To understand
the universe

2. To acquire power

Match the purpose

Can you imagine Disney recruiting the kind of livewires that currently make up the company on the basis of the purpose 'to make consistent profits'? Can you imagine the kind of quality of movies that would produce? Can you imagine what kind of deadheads would be applying to work at Disney under those circumstances?

A purpose, once identified, requires no justification. Others either buy into it or they get out. If you find yourself or others justifying the purpose, you probably have not identified your purpose.

- Sony – 'to experience the joy of advancing and applying technology for the benefit of the public'

This is a rather long and clumsy phrasal verb (what you have just read has been considerably shortened; the original was even more complex and unwieldy), but it is in the spirit of a purpose. However, it may be too long and complex to easily keep in mind. Had Sony followed it, they would not have had the fiasco with the Betamax video system. They would have done what JVC did: enable anyone who wanted a licence to manufacture their product to do so. What happened? JVC cornered the world-wide market on video technology even though, as many technical commentators have noted, Betamax was a superior product. Moral of the story – keep your purpose statement short and simple enough for everyone to remember it, understand it and use it.

SUMMARY

Purpose is that which the organisation will always be doing. Purpose, along with an organisation's values, are the core of what the organisation is; they are central to who you are. Purpose and values are the 'why' of an organisation.

VALUES

VALUES DEFINED

Values are the core beliefs the organisation actually holds or wishes to hold (and is not prepared to compromise under any circumstances).

STATUS IN THE CAM

Values, along with purpose, make up 'who you are', why the organisation exists.

WHAT DO VALUES DO?

They provide guidance and a common reference point to make decisions.

PREFERRED FORM OF EXPRESSION

It is possible to complete the sentence 'We value ...' using an attribute (not an object) without creating any grammatical anomalies.

VALUES EXPANDED

Values are the guiding philosophy of any organisation, and are usually put in place by the founder, or may be distilled and instilled by the current leader.

> The glue which holds a company together is its beliefs and values rather than its structures and systems. (Sir Adrian Cadbury)

Shared values are enormous time-savers. Have you ever sat on a board (or any other committee) which has no clearly articulated and shared values. It is a nightmare! Proposals are presented, the debate starts. One person objects to it for one reason, and someone else supports it for exactly the same reason. A third party suggests it should be held over for further consideration for the same reason that the other two wanted to block or support it. Then someone introduces another value, and the same agreement/disagreement/neutral posturing starts all over again.

Obviously, I am simplifying the degree of chaos for the purposes of conveying the point, but you've been there, you've seen it, you know it goes on and on and on and nothing is decided. Why? Because there are no agreed values; there is rarely a clearly spelled out vision. Sure, there are plenty of laudable platitudes flying around, but nothing of substance that people can use for guidance. And what happens in the absence of a clear and agreed set of values to use for guidance? People use their own personal values. When you have a group of individuals with only their own personal values for guidance, what happens. Two things: chaos, and not a lot else.

> The leader's role is to distil and to instil values. (Sir Adrian Cadbury)

41

Values are distinct from purpose in that values express who you are and what you stand for, whereas purpose expresses why you are, what you exist to do. Here are some examples of values used by extremely successful organisations and people:

- IBM – respect for the individual; major attention to service; superiority in all things
- WL Gore (Goretex) – fairness; mutual development; self-responsibility; information-sharing
- Hewlett Packard – respect for individuals; dedication to affordable quality; commitment to community responsibility; advancement and welfare of humanity
- Founding Fathers (USA) – one of the first things they did was to agree the US Constitution: a list of values by which everything else in the new country would be decided (probably the wisest group of people at any one place at one time in all human history!)
- French Revolution – liberty; equality; fraternity
- Ghandi (India) – peaceful, passive resistance proved devastatingly effective, so much so that many major 'revolutions' since his time have been achieved by drawing on that value and the behaviours which follow from it (e.g., in the Philippines in the 1980s and most former Soviet Bloc countries in the 1990s)
- Martin Luther King (USA) – King modelled Ghandi's success and lived by

the same values; those values were adopted as the Civil Rights Movement got up to full speed in the USA

- Nelson Mandela (South Africa) – most people know that all Mandela had to do to be released from prison many years before that eventually happened was to renounce violence as a means of struggle. Why is he held in such high esteem throughout the world? Because he held and holds justice for all as a value above all other values, even that of his own freedom. How can we help but follow such an example?

- China – earlier on I mentioned the memes which have governed Chinese society for 2 500 years; I'm not sure how Confucius would have turned his principles of government into a values list, but here is my attempt: meritocracy; economic control; utilisation of surplus; information control. Whether you approve or disapprove (as I do) of these values, there can be no denying that they have held together the largest population in the world for over 2 000 years. The Chinese are by far the longest surviving mass civilisation in the world today.

- Winston Churchill (Britain, World War II) – liberty; justice; freedom

In 1940, spelling out the most important of the UK's values when he first took office, Churchill said in the House of Commons:

> I speak to you for the first time as Prime Minister in this solemn hour for the life of our country, of our empire, of our allies, and above all, of the cause of *freedom*.

This is perhaps the most famous of all value-reinforcement speeches, although at no point did he need to state what values he was referring to. From all his previous speeches, everyone listening knew that he was referring to freedom, and that the young men who fought and died for that freedom were protecting something much, much more important than a small island:

> Never in the field of human conflict has so much been owed by so many to so few.

Hundreds of times I have read those words, and they still send a shiver down my spine and bring tears to my eyes. Why? Because I, too, passionately believe in democratic freedom, and I can imagine the mix of passion and fear that drove those youngsters to stand up for what is just and be prepared to take the consequences.

That is the kind of spirit that achieves wonderful things. That is the kind of spirit that all wise business leaders would like to harness, yet sadly, many of them set goals more likely to send people cold: 'Increase shareholder value'; 'Double our return on capital'; 'Make more profit.'

When, oh when, will they get the message? People do not jump out of bed blazing with passion to put more money in shareholders' pockets. People do not spend their weekends dreaming up ways to double return on capital. All of those types of effects happen as a side-effect of achieving something awesome. Give people something exciting, and they will give you all the boring but necessary things on their way to what really matters to them. At the risk of substituting one platitude for another: shareholder value is increased when customer needs are met in a way that no one else can meet them.

Exercise: What are the values of your organisation? Are they clearly articulated and documented? Are they known and used by one and all?

SUMMARY

Noble values bring out the best in people. People work to realise values they hold highly. People will go to extraordinary lengths to defend and perpetuate values they believe in. People are guided by values. People bond and unite around values. People align in the direction of shared values. People's behaviour is determined by their values. People's collective behaviour is determined by their values. The future of your organisation is determined by how well you can align your people behind a set of shared values.

DIRECTION

DIRECTION DEFINED

Direction is the road along which you choose to travel in pursuit of your purpose. Or phrased more comfortably: direction – the road along which the purpose will be pursued.

STATUS IN THE CAM

Direction is the 1st-level 'what to'.

WHAT DOES DIRECTION DO?

It specifies which of the many possible routes to pursuing a purpose will be chosen. It often has the the effect of specifying, at the highest possible level, the marketplace in which you will operate.

SOME DIRECTION EXAMPLES

- 3M's purpose – 'to solve unsolved problems'
- 3M's direction – technology problems (technological as opposed to methodological or social or political problems)

- Disney's purpose – 'to make people happy'
- Disney's direction – entertainment (as opposed to many other possible directions)

- MacLennan's purpose – 'to improve mental effectiveness'
- MacLennan's direction – business-thinking effectiveness (methodological as opposed to technological, social or political effectiveness)

Going down the hierarchy, this is the first level we have reached that can be changed without trying to change the entire organisational culture. You can continue to hold the same values, have the same *raison d'être* and still change your direction. You can choose to make people happy through entertainment as a direction. You can choose to do it through finance. You can choose to do it by providing homes. You can do it in no end of ways. You can choose to solve unsolved problems in the direction of technology, or in methodology or in politics, and so on.

You can keep your values and purpose intact, but still change direction. You can look at pursuing your purpose with your values in the direction of another market.

Exercise: In which direction is your organisation pursuing its purpose? Is it articulated? Is it shared? Is it documented?

VISION

VISION DEFINED

Vision has an end point eight to twenty-five years in the future: the most distant future and (possibly) achievable manifestation of your purpose you can see along the direction you have chosen.

STATUS IN THE CAM

This is also part of the 2nd-level or long-term 'what to'.

WHAT DOES VISION DO?

Having such a long-term target provides a distant benchmark against which everyone in the company can make decisions. It gives staff:

- the means to interpret day-to-day activities in terms of a higher-level goal
- a focus for their activity
- a means by which to make decisions
- a clear picture of what the organisation will look like
- a sense of being involved in something worthwhile
- a benchmark against which to gauge their efforts

The stronger the vision, the more each of the above benefits will apply.

Without a vision, people become activity-focused; agenda- rather than objectives-driven. Without a vision, people have no means by which to judge their contribution, and managers have no means by which to set outcome measures. Without a clear vision, people have no means by which to resolve the dilemmas presented to them on a daily basis. The weaker the vision, the more these problems will be evident.

PREFERRED FORM OF EXPRESSION

Vision must conjure up a specific picture of the end point in the minds of those at whom it is aimed. There are many possible ways of doing this:

> Vision is central to ensuring that everyone in an organisation knows what the goals of an enterprise are and how their particular job contributes to them. (Sir Adrian Cadbury)

> A vision is only seen if everyone is looking in the same direction.

> Vision must be communicable, coherent, comprehensible, communicated and captivating.

VISION EXPANDED

Let's look at an example of one of the best-presented visions in history. Martin Luther King, spelling out a vision for all America and the world on racial equality at the Lincoln Memorial in Washington in 1963, said:

> I have a dream that one day even the State of Mississippi, a desert sweltering with the heat of injustice and oppression ... will be transformed into an oasis of freedom and justice ... I have a dream that my four little children ... will one day live in a nation where they will not be judged by the colour of their skin but by the content of their character ... I have a dream today. I have a dream ...

If that has not persuaded you that visions must be inspiring, perhaps this quotation of his from 1968, restating the vision in the face of multiple barriers and even threats to his life a few hours before his assassination, will:

> I just want to do God's will. And he has allowed me to go up to the mountain top. And I have looked over. And I have seen the promised land. I may not get there with you. But I want you to know tonight that we as a people will get to the promised land.

Within a very short period, black segregation in the USA was outlawed, and some years after that, 'Martin Luther King Day' was created in memory of the man and as a symbol aimed at further promoting racial harmony. Just over twenty-five years later, apartheid fell in South Africa. The vision created by that man lives on today, long after his death.

The 'common or garden' zip

You probably read these words within at most a few metres of a zip. Its simple principle was the realisation of a vision lasting fourteen years. Gideon Sundback (why is his name not a household name, given the ubiquity of his invention?) had a clear picture of what he wanted to achieve. At that time, the existing method of fastening clothing was the button. Buttoning requires each hole to be cut, and the surrounding material must then be stitched. Buttons must be manufactured, they must be positioned and sewn. Once in place, the buttons must be fastened and unfastened individually – a task requiring a reasonable degree of dexterity. Not easy if you are cold, wrapped up, elderly or in one of a whole host of other human conditions which make buttoning difficult.

Gideon Sundback's vision was to create a means of fastening material which was superior to the button. He wanted something which was quick and easy to use. He had many, many false starts. He tried all sorts of methods. Even when he stumbled across the one which was ultimately to work, he still had to find a way through many, many barriers to arrive at his destination. Without that clear vision, he would never have got there.

We could fill the rest of this book with case histories of people and companies who had a clear vision and pursued it to the point of completion. Most great human advances were not the subject of some instant creation. Most were the result of a few people holding in their minds a picture of what they wanted their end point to look like. They did not and could not have known the specifics of how they would achieve the vision, but hold it they did. Hold one you must.

You don't have to be as good an orator as Martin Luther King. You don't have to have a vision that seeks realisation in as ubiquitous a way as Gideon Sundback's. (But if you have both these things, your competition might as well liquidate now. For you will align your company behind a single worthwhile focus that all your staff believe in.) You simply must be prepared to work with your staff at coming up with a great vision. You simply must be prepared to work at finding a great way of communicating that vision. You will see how shortly.

Exercise: What is your organisation's great vision? What point have your CEO and board stated that you are trying to reach in the long-term future? How is that great vision communicated?

SUMMARY

For any great achievement to take place, there must be a strong, clear vision on which those involved can focus. What makes a good vision? A vision that is too complex is as impotent as no vision at all. It should form a single picture which defines a definite end point or target. An ideal vision should involve people in some wonderful human advance.

MISSION

MISSION DEFINED

A mission has an end point three to eight years in the future: the mid-term achievable manifestation of your vision.

STATUS IN THE CAM

This is the mid-term part of the 3rd-level 'what to'.

WHAT DOES A MISSION DO?

Having a mid-term target provides a more immediate benchmark against which everyone in the company can make decisions.

Both visions and missions erect goalposts for your team to aim for. Continuing the soccer analogy, the mission statement provides a goal that must be scored before your team are allowed access to the vision goal. In other words, you must score the mission goal before qualifying for the next round, when the vision goal becomes the focus. A mission is always a more immediate focal point than a vision.

Both vision and mission are useless unless all those whose co-operation is required to achieve them think it is a worthwhile endeavour into which they are prepared to pour their energies.

Most managers cannot quote their company mission. Go on, humour me, go for a wander around your business and ask the first fifty managers you meet. I guarantee that if your mission statement is more than nine words long, less than 20 per cent of the people you meet will be able to recite it. As the number of words increases to over thirty or more, I will bet that you can find no one other than its author(s) who can quote it. If fifty managers cannot quote it, what chance is there that lower-level managers or staff can? If people cannot remember a mission, how do you expect them to live it?

PREFERRED FORM OF EXPRESSION

A mission must contain a visualisable end point.

EXAMPLES OF GREAT MISSIONS

- John F. Kennedy (mission-setting, 1962) – 'We will put a man on the moon by the end of this decade.'
- Neil Armstrong (mission-completing, 1969) – 'One small step for a man, one giant leap for mankind.' (as it was intended to have been said)

Both visions and mission must be communicated regularly, particularly in the face of events which may make it appear that the mission is less likely to be realised, or in the face of events which may make it appear that the vision or mission have been completed when they have not.

- Churchill: 'We will defend our island, whatever the cost may be.'
  'This is not the end. It is not even the beginning of the end, but it is the end of the beginning.'

Here are some more examples of missions:

- Komatsu: 'To encircle Caterpillar' (their biggest competitor)
- British Airways: 'To be the world's favourite airline.'
- TSB Bank: 'To be the UK's leading financial retailer.'

Which of these do you think satisfy the condition stated so far for an effective mission statement, that it must contain a visualisable end point?

Some mission statements are actually purpose statements, for instance:

We are in the business of preserving human life. (Merck, USA, healthcare)
To promote the art and science of management. (The Institute of Management, UK)

Why are these purpose statements? Because they can be engaged in perpetually. They are rather good – no, perfect – examples of purpose statements, but they are not mission statements. Why not? Because they have no manifestable end points. They have no 'we know when we have achieved that' indicator required for a good mission statement.

You may say: 'They are successful organisations. Confusing a purpose statement with a mission statement can't be that serious.' You would be right. Having a mission statement, no matter how bad, may make you better than the vast majority of organisations in the world. But presumably you are not reading this chapter or this book to be a little better than dismal. You are, I hope, reading this to be the best. Think how much better those organisations could be if their mission statement actually told their staff what their mid-term target was as well as completely stating the purpose?

Exercise: Take a look at your current mission statement, if you have one. Does it state a clear mid-term target?

STRATEGY

We are going to break off briefly here to make an important point.

One of the many reasons that the terms used in business cause regular confusion is that the same word is used to mean many things. For instance, 'strategy' is used to mean different things at least three different levels in organisational life. At the highest level, it is often used to mean 'purpose'. At the competitive level, it is used to mean the method of attack in the marketplace. At the middle management level, it is often used to mean 'tactic'. At the operational level, it is used to mean 'operating principles'. For that reason, this term and all others central to the CAM have been clearly defined.

So in what ways could we define strategy? Here are a few:

1. Strategy is individual or group behaviour aimed at securing some competitive advantage.
2. Strategy is the means of delivering your core competence to your chosen marketplace.
3. Strategy is the management of mission.
4. Strategy is the way an organisation harnesses its resources to deliver something that its customers find attractive.

All of the above statements have some truth in them. Most have something lacking. The one that comes closest to a usable definition is number 4.

The following is the best and most understandable definition I've been able to come up with (there is always a conflict between academically rigorous definitions and those that are usable in the real world). .

STRATEGY DEFINED

Strategy is the means by which the organisation's resources are brought to bear on, and found to be attractive by, the target market to achieve the mission. (Note that 'target market' also means customer's desires, whosoever may be the customer.)

STATUS IN THE CAM

Strategy is the 1st-level 'how to'.

WHAT DOES STRATEGY DO, IN TERMS OF TEAM ALIGNMENT?

Knowing the means by which resources are being brought to bear gives everyone a high-level guide on making decisions about 'how to'.

PREFERRED FORM OF EXPRESSION

Like purpose, a strategy statement can be expressed as 'never-ending', the difference being that a strategy will continue only as long as the marketplace values the 'how to' behind it. As soon as the market changes its 'how to' preference, a strategy is up for renewal. The apparently never-ending nature of strategy expressed in a similar way to a purpose is the main reason the two are confused, even amongst top-level business-educated and experienced people.

As before, an example illustrates a thousand explanations (and as before, some have been altered to make sense out of context and to fit into a standard format):

- Intel – 'produce increasingly superior microchip technology'
- Microsoft – 'provide the best standardised software elements in computing' (one part)
- Microsoft –'provide the easiest access to the electronic entertainment people want to have' (another part)
- Rally's (a McDonald's competitor) – 'provide the fastest fast food in the fast food industry'
- Marks & Spencer – 'provide the highest possible quality at the lowest possible cost'
- Virgin Pensions – 'provide pensions with the lowest possible overhead charges'
- Nike – 'provide sportswear with the strongest association with sports achievement'
- Boeing – 'provide the fastest delivery at the lowest cost'

STRATEGY EXPANDED

For a strategy to be effective, it must be understood by all those contributing to it. If your people don't know the means by which you are seeking to deliver what the customer wants, how can they help you to do so? Even if everyone knows it and applies it, your strategy must be in tune with your values and purpose to be delivered effectively. A theoretically right strategy works only when conduct is the consequence of belief. In other words: the strategy must be drawn from your values and purpose.

The values, purpose and vision of an organisation can be seen or inferred from a good strategy. In fact, a purpose, vision and strategy can be crystallised into one phrase, into one awesome purpose. That is the ideal.

You might ask: 'How many strategies can an organisation have?' Ideally one, and only one. At the start of this section I pointed out the confusion caused by companies using 'strategy' to mean different things at different levels in the organisation. All organisations should have only one strategy. 'Ah, but,' you might say, 'what if the organisation has several divisions, each of which are independent?' Good point. If each division is truly independent and functions as an organisation in its own right, it should have its own strategy.

If two separate strategies are emerging in an organisation, you should be thinking of creating two separate organisations. No organisation can serve two separate means of bringing its resources to bear and not end up riven by conflict and confusion; there should be only one strategy per organisation.

Exercise: What is your organisation's current strategy? Where is it documented? Ask twenty managers to state your organisation's strategy. No prompting. If you have an aligned culture, you will get twenty identical answers. The fewer identical answers you get, the more alignment is required.

MAJOR OBJECTIVES

MAJOR OBJECTIVES DEFINED

Major objectives are the key targets which will have to be achieved using the strategy if the mission is to be successful.

STATUS IN THE CAM

This is the 4th-level 'what to'.

WHAT DO MAJOR OBJECTIVES DO?

Setting the major objectives gives people an even more immediate benchmark (than the mission) against which to make decisions. On the occasions in which the major objectives prove inconclusive as a decision-making guide, reference can be made to the higher-level 'what tos': mission and vision.

PREFERRED FORM OF EXPRESSION

As long as they follow the SMART principles, they will probably be OK – major objectives should be:

- Specific
- Measured
- Achievable
- Realistic
- Timed

EXAMPLES OF SOME MAJOR OBJECTIVES

- Boeing – 'reduce the time to manufacture a plane from 18 months to 8 months in four years; reduce costs by 25 per cent in six years'
- 3M – 'generate 30 per cent of revenues from products which did not exist four years ago'

Can you list your organisation's major objectives, those that are dictated by the strategy to achieve the mission? Probably. For that reason, I will be providing less detail at the lower levels of the CAM. Objective-setting was well covered by Drucker over forty years ago, and is now well taught at most business schools and on professional courses (see *The Practice of Management*, Drucker 1954).

TACTICS

TACTICS DEFINED

Tactics are the micro-methods used to achieve the major objectives drawn from the strategy.

STATUS IN THE CAM

This is the 2nd-level 'how to': tactics are the interpretations of strategy at functional levels.

WHAT DO TACTICS DO?

They provide 'how to achieve the major objectives' guidance.

Strategy is often too blunt an instrument with which to make day-to-day micro-level decisions. Strategy has different manifestations for the various functional groupings within any organisation. Spelling out the tactics as they apply to each grouping gives them a means to focus their efforts and the 'how to' on a local scale. Tactics are the interpretations of strategy at functional levels: the short-term components of strategy (the methods by which the major objectives, derived from the strategy and the higher elements in the CAM, are achieved).

SOME EXAMPLES

If speed of service is your strategy, then the methods your marketing team use to convey that to your potential customers are tactics. The methods your operations people use to deliver quickly are tactics. The means your order-processing people use to clear the order and put it in the hands of your operations people are tactics.

If your strategy is to provide the best in your field and charge according to that superiority, it might be smart to restrict supply of your product to ensure thatyour demand, and therefore prices, stay up. Nintendo are thought to have

restricted the supply of its computer games to keep up demand, maintain prices and keep the balance of power between themselves and retailers tilted in their favour. When people are queuing outside your retail store for a supplier's game, you don't force your suppliers to drop their prices, do you? When you *have* to get a product for your family because it is so good, you can't really start haggling or going elsewhere, can you? Or at least, not until there is a better product available.

Exercise: List the tactics your department uses to deliver your major objectives.

OBJECTIVES

OBJECTIVES DEFINED

Objectives are the steps required to achieve the major objectives using the tactics chosen.

STATUS IN THE CAM

This is the 5th-level 'what to'.

WHAT DO OBJECTIVES DO?

They establish clearly what staff are expected to do on an immediate basis.

Well-run companies are objectives- and outcomes-driven; and both are derived from major objectives. They, in turn, are derived from the strategy; that is derived from what the customer wants and your awesome purpose. All are derived in line with your values.

Poorly run companies are agenda-driven. Meetings are dominated by going through the sequence on the agenda.

Poorly run companies are budget-driven. Activities are centred around fulfilling the budget commitments. Managers are more interested in making sure their budget forecasts are met than in delivering benefit to customers. The decisions made in the last budget round nearly a year ago are used to make decisions, in preference to the customer-provided information of today. Little wonder their customers look out for better suppliers until they find them.

Poorly run companies are process-driven. They allow the process to be more important than that for which the process was created: an outcome, a deliverable. Academics are notorious for this. Each year they produce millions of perfectly written papers in thousands of journals, and less than one in ten thousand actually achieves any kind of outcome.

Exercise: Take the major objective that applies to your function or department, and list the objectives that have been set to achieve that major objective.

OPERATING PRINCIPLES

OPERATING PRINCIPLES DEFINED

Operating principles are 'how tos' which apply to achieving objectives: the localised interpretation of tactics.

STATUS IN THE CAM

This is the 3rd-level 'how to'.

WHAT DO OPERATING PRINCIPLES DO?

They provide guidelines which are used to make day-to-day decisions about how to achieve your objectives.

In the same way that tactics are the localised 'how to' interpretation of the strategy, operating principles are the localised 'how to' interpretation of tactics.

You may find that you have the same operating principles being used throughout the company. That is one reason why most people confuse values with operating principles. Each department does not need to have its own unique operating principles. They can be shared; but that does not make them values. The same operating principles may be in place throughout the company, based on the shared values, but that does not make them the same thing. Your strategy will almost certainly draw on your values, but would that lead you to say strategy is the same as values? Of course not.

CLARIFYING THE DISTINCTION BETWEEN OPERATING PRINCIPLES AND TACTICS

For example, providing the highest possible quality in a particular customer deliverable may be an operating principle driven by a current demand by customers. However, if one of your values is 'giving the customer what they want' and customers start demanding lower prices for lower-quality goods, you'll drop quality as an operating principle instantly.

Exercise: What are your operating principles? In the department with which you have most contact, list the operating principles that are used to guide staff activities.

5 Using the CAM

CHAPTER OVERVIEW

- A reminder of the power of culture
  - Things go wrong
- Great leadership and culture
- To CAM, or not to CAM?
- The status quo
- An idealised and complete CAM example
- 'Why?', 'What?' and 'How?'
- How long does alignment/change take?
- Values and purpose: The backbone of culture

Now we have covered the basics of the CAM, we should go on to show you how to use it, show you the tools you need to make it work, explore where awesome purpose sits in the CAM, and then where the CAM sits in the 9 Rs of alignment.

Remember that the CAM is a model and framework for creating alignment or facilitating change. It is the basis for making sure everyone knows what the culture is and what they are buying into, and, perhaps most importantly, it gives people the means by which to decide if they can or cannot buy into the culture (if not, they have to go). It is the means by which you can coach the culture so that, in turn, the culture will coach your people.

A REMINDER OF THE POWER OF CULTURE

Values, purpose, vision, mission, direction and strategy, once articulated, communicated and shared, provide a framework for self-control and decision-making. That, in turn, removes the need for all the heavy-handed control structures usually seen in organisations characterised by lack of clear cultural alignment.

An aligned culture and an awesome purpose (or at least a clear, shared vision) make it possible for every member of staff to ask themselves how they contribute to the realisation of the vision. A clear strategy enables them to assess the ways in which they contribute to the 'how to'. In short, once staff know the rules of the working environment and they know the 'what to' and the 'how to', they are in a position to judge how to make their maximum contribution to the organisation. Without that knowledge, whether provided in the format of the CAM or not, how can staff possibly make decisions about how to contribute effectively? How can they possibly fill in the inevitable gaps in their bosses' instructions?

THINGS GO WRONG

The unpredictable will predictably happen. When it does, it reveals one of the hallmarks of a strong culture: the ability to cope with the unpredictable. Because everyone has a shared set of values, because everyone is driven by the same awesome purpose, everyone has the same set of guidelines to handle any crisis.

How do your staff handle crises?

Exercise: When things go wrong in your current organisation, how do you and your staff handle the problem? What framework or guidelines do you look to? Do your staff do that without reference to their boss? If so, you have a great culture. If not, you have a classic symptom of a poorly aligned culture.

GREAT LEADERSHIP AND CULTURE

The highest level of leadership is the management of the way the organisation is managed. That means ensuring there is a clear vision and a strong culture. Great leaders coach rather than control. Great leaders set up the culture to provide guidelines for all in that culture. Great leaders coach their managers to manage the culture and their part in the achievement of the vision. Great leaders are the custodians or creators of their organisational cultures; they know that if they manage the culture, the culture will manage the company.

Another hallmark of good leadership includes removing the obstacles that prevent managers from performing, such as things which muddy the cultural clarity they and you seek.

TO CAM, OR NOT TO CAM?

Your cultural alignment method need not follow the CAM exactly; your definitions of vision or mission may vary from mine (although you must have shared definitions), but all the principles behind the elements of the model must be in place, by design or default, if you are to stand any chance of success in your culture change/alignment/creation.

Exercise: What model is used in your organisation to align the culture. If you do not have one, what does that tell you?

THE STATUS QUO

Most companies currently have the following.

THE 'WHY'

- **Purpose** – There is probably no defined purpose.
- **Values** – There are probably no clearly defined values. If they do exist, there will be too many to remember, or they will be espoused and not actual, or they will be meaningless platitudes.

LEVEL 1

- **Direction** – Almost always a company has a direction (usually by default), but very rarely is it articulated even at the highest levels in the most sophisticated companies.
- **Vision** – There is probably no clear vision. If one does exist, it will be too long, too complex, eminently forgettable and non-visual. In many cases it will be all of the above and worse.
- **Mission** – Yes, you probably have one, but it can't be remembered by your staff. It is likely to be a mismatch of values, purpose, operating principles and a host of other non-mission-related platitudes.
- **Strategy** – Yes, you probably have one, but do your staff know it? If I were

59

to call your business and ask the first ten people to whom I spoke if they could tell me what your strategy is, could they do so? Probably not. And if a few senior managers could, would it be expressed in such long and convoluted terms that you have probably had approaches from some drug companies looking to use it as a successor to their top brand of sleeping tablets? If you do have a clear and concise strategy and you think I'm being flippant, call a few of your suppliers or customers and ask them what their strategy is.

LEVEL 2

- **Major objectives** – You probably have a list of major objectives. Even the worst companies have. Unfortunately, they may not be documented and distributed to those who are charged with achieving them. And if they are, they are not usually specific, measurable, achievable, realistic or timed.
- **Tactics** – As with most of the lower levels in the CAM, many companies have something close to each specified element, but only in the minds of the top team. Those who most need to know are not informed.

LEVEL 3

- **Objectives** – At the bottom of the commercial food-chain, setting SMART objectives is too much to expect. Most larger companies, no matter how badly managed, are able to set objectives. Whether they qualify as SMART objectives is another matter.
- **Operating principles** – It is almost impossible to do anything for any period without a set of operating principles being established. Whether those are articulated is quite a different matter. Few organisations establish and communicate their operating principles to those who need to know them.

Exercise: Be honest now: how does your company compare to the list above? Did you see yourself, or a large part of yourself?

AN IDEALISED AND COMPLETE CAM EXAMPLE

OK, enough criticism; it's time to deliver. What does a properly completed CAM look like? Here is an idealised complete example for a company which manufactures instruments.

THE 'WHY'

- **Values** – integrity, empowerment, development
- **Purpose** – to enable people to measure whatever they want or need to

LEVEL 1

- **Direction** – They could make medical instruments, aviation instruments, domestic instruments, automotive instruments, and may in time make all of these. Initially, they must choose a direction. The direction which they believe matches their values is the industrial instrument direction.
- **Vision** – Every industrial measurement instrument can be instantly installed and be maintenance-free.
- **Mission** – To provide the fastest-installed and lowest-maintenance industrial measurement instruments in the world.
- **Strategy** – Progressively lower the total cost of industrial measurement instruments.

LEVEL 2

- **Major objectives** – (to conserve space, we are going to follow only one major objective) Reduce the failure rate of our instruments by 10 per cent per annum.
- **Tactics** – Use the Pareto Principle (to make the greatest impact in the shortest possible time).

LEVEL 3

- **Objectives** – (1) Identify the 20 per cent of causes that account for the 80 per cent of failures. (2) Identify or create a range of methods to remove or cure the failure causes identified above. (3) Identify the total cost of implementing the best solutions to the above failures. (4) Identify those solutions which provide 80 per cent of the improvement at 20 per cent of the cost calculated above, etc.
- **Operating principles** – (1) 80 per cent of the information required will be available from 20 per cent of the sources. (2) Use published and already existing sources of information first. (3) Harness that which works best.

AWESOME PURPOSE

- Instant, maintenance-free measurement.

Exercise: How does your company compare to this one? How many elements from the list above can you complete in your company?

'WHY?', 'WHAT?' AND 'HOW?'

If you look at the CAM you can see that (in simplistic terms) it can be divided into layers which correspond to the three levels of management: senior, middle and junior. You could say that each level requires you to answer three questions: 'Why?', 'What?' and 'How?' The answers to the top-level 'Why?', 'What to?' and 'How to?' set the parameters for the middle level, and that sets the boundaries for the junior level. Each level shares the same 'why' (the diagram below sets out the relationship between the elements of the CAM).

The relationship between the elements of the CAM
© 1998 N.T.R. MacLennan

If you are looking for a simpler model than the CAM, then the 'Why? What to? How to?' approach might seem tempting. Simply, you might think, get your whole company to answer the 'Why? What to? How to?' sequence and you could use that as the basis of your cultural alignment. Maybe. If you lead a small organisation with only one layer of management, such an approach might well work.

But if your organisation is multi-layered, it won't work easily. The danger with this simplistic approach is that it creates no distinction between strategy and tactics, no distinction between vision and objectives, no distinction between values and operating principles, and so on. You have a senior manager's 'how', a junior manager's 'how', a director's 'what' and a middle manager's 'what'. Each level in the organisation must have its own interpretation of the vision, one that is appropriate to their contribution to the vision. If you have the same terms (why, what, how) being used to describe different goals and methods, confusion of the kind you are trying to remove is introduced.

HOW LONG DOES ALIGNMENT/CHANGE TAKE?

Companies consistently underestimate how much time and effort effective and lasting change entails. It is always much more time than you hope: anything between eighteen months and ten years. It always takes much, much more effort than you hope. Nearly all of your senior staff will dedicate about 60–80 per cent of their time to the change project for as long as it lasts – assuming you want change to be successful, of course.

Let's clear up some commonly reported confusions between terms:

- **Mission and vision are different** – Visions are achievable in eight to twenty-five years; missions are mid-term targets, three to eight years.
- **Strategy and tactics are different** – Tactics are the local or functional interpretation of the organisation-wide strategy.
- **Tactics and operating principles are different** – Operating principles are the departmental interpretation of functional tactics.
- **Operating principles and values are different** – Values are part of who you are and are immutable; an operating principle is a method currently adopted to achieve an objective (operating principles often become so permanent and central to a business that they are confused with, and assumed to be, values).
- **Purpose and vision are different** – Purpose is what you will always be doing; vision is a definable milestone on the never-ending road to that purpose.
- **Mission and direction are different** – Direction is the road along which you choose to travel in order to pursue your purpose; mission is a mid-term milestone along that road.
- **Values and purpose** – These are the central parts of any successful culture. Before I go on to show how to arrive at them, let's spend a little time looking at their role and source.

VALUES AND PURPOSE: THE BACKBONE OF CULTURE

Values and purpose are not created, they are uncovered. They existed in the minds of the business founders, and have evolved over time as the business has passed from one group of caretakers to another.

Values and purpose can be identical in several companies. Values and purpose guide rather than differentiate. Differentiation comes from the manifestation of values and purpose at the lower levels in the CAM. It comes from the direction, vision, mission and strategy of the organisation.

Some people assume that a strong set of shared values and a unifying purpose translates in reality into a highly conforming culture. It can, but only if one of the actual values (as opposed to espoused values) is 'following the rules'. And that usually means doing things in a prescribed way, and only in that way: decision-making power is taken out of the hands of staff and managers. A well-aligned culture does not look like a group of compliant clones, it is a voluntary gathering of people adhering to a set of values they all agree with; it is a group of people who use those values as guidelines for their own decision-making.

The people in those companies have chosen to be there because they held the shared values before they joined the company. That was one of the things that attracted them to the company in the first place. Not all companies are so fortunate. Few cultures are so well aligned. Perhaps you are thinking, 'That's all very well, but I inherited a company where there are no shared values. I can't just impose a set of values on the staff.' Of course, you would be right. You can't just impose a set of values on the staff, and you may well have no clear set of values. But does that mean that you cannot start moving towards having a shared set of values? Does it also mean that you can't distil what common values do exist, and seek to keep the best and change the worst by setting up reward and decision-making systems in line with the values you do want the company to live? No. Even if your company is an anarchists' playground, you are not powerless to make cultural changes.

Once you have made some noticeable changes, once you have distilled and communicated your company's values and purpose, you will find the process takes on a life of its own. You will start to attract those who are compatible and reject those who are not. Yes, that does mean you will lose some members of staff and some managers. But, in their place, you will gain those who share your values, who want to live your purpose, who want to join your crusade. The quasi-religious language was not used by accident. People want to be part of some worthy cause; provide that for them, and they will provide what you need. Let's look at how to do that.

Building a truly awesome company takes one part vision and a thousand parts alignment.

Exercise: Spend a few minutes answering the following three questions. How do I determine my company's purpose? How do I distil my company's values? How do I create an awesome purpose?

6 Completing the CAM

CHAPTER OVERVIEW

- The 9R Model
- Establishing the 'why'
- The purpose–values link
- Identifying your values
- Deciding what values to formally adopt
- Value–purpose match
- Putting the adopted values in place
- Checking that the values have been adopted
- Summary

What is meant by 'completing the CAM'? Specifying what each of the terms in the CAM means in your organisation:

1. Distil your organisation's purpose.
2. Establish its values.
3. Determine the direction in which it is travelling to pursue the purpose.
4. Pull together a long-term goal (a vision), a mid-term goal (a mission) and an electrifying goal (an awesome purpose).
5. Determine your organisation's strategy.
6. Establish the major objectives.
7. Determine the tactics to deliver each of the major objectives.
8. Set objectives.
9. Determine your operating principles.
10. Develop the awesome purpose.

As you probably noticed, you can also develop the awesome purpose in stage 4 above. Whether to work on the awesome purpose in stage 4 or stage 10 creates a dilemma. Do you come up with an awesome purpose as early in the process as possible to inspire your staff to complete the rest of the CAM, or do you get as many people as possible involved in completing the CAM before drawing on that organisational unity to distil an awesome purpose? In most of the cases I have been involved with or know of, the organisation's leaders have chosen to generate their awesome purpose after having established purpose, values, direction, vision, mission and strategy. That is when they have completed everything in the 'why' and Level 1.

THE 9R MODEL

Before we look at determining purpose, establishing values, compiling a vision, and so on, we should place these activities in some form of context.

You seek to align or change your culture. The CAM is the tool for the job. Like most tools, there is a sequence of steps for using it effectively. That sequence is the '9 Rs'. For any application of the CAM to be successful, you must follow the 9R steps (to avoid distracting attention from the central message, only the Re-visioning stage is explained below):

1. **Realisation**
2. **Rallying**
3. **Recognition**
4. **Reframing**
5. **Re-visioning** – completing the CAM, and agreeing an awesome purpose
6. **Redesigning**
7. **Re-aligning**
8. **Revising**
9. **Retaining**

Since we are in the middle of explaining the CAM and it is fresh in your mind, it seems better to demonstrate how to conduct the activities which take place in the Re-visioning stage now, rather than waiting until we go through the 9 Rs in detail.

ESTABLISHING THE 'WHY'

IDENTIFYING YOUR PURPOSE

Purpose: that which the organisation will always be doing.

The objective of this section is to enable you to answer the question: 'How do I determine my company's purpose?'

Here are a range of tools to help you establish a purpose.

USE THE 'WHY?' CHAIN

Have you ever been intellectually cornered by a curious kid? They ask you about something, you give an answer you hope is within their sphere of understanding. They look at you and simply ask 'Why?' You do the same again. They make the same move again, and within six steps, it is checkmate: a fully-grown, supremely well-educated adult reduced to frustrated, inarticulate and moronic mumblings by a pre-schooler. 'From the mouths of babes . . .'

How can we harness that phenomenon? Take the process back to the answer you gave just before checkmate, and you have probably identified the pinnacle of your knowledge on whatever the subject was. Let's apply that to a business context. State what it is the company produces (by product or service category) and ask, 'Why should we do that?', or simply, 'We do ABC. Why?' And keep asking 'Why?' Ask the 'Why?' chain of as many people in your organisation as you can before one of them gives you a black eye. Eventually, you get to one which sounds like 'to advance human life', the one beyond that is the one that gets you the black eye. Take the answer immediately prior to 'advance human life': that will be that person's best definition of the purpose for what they do.

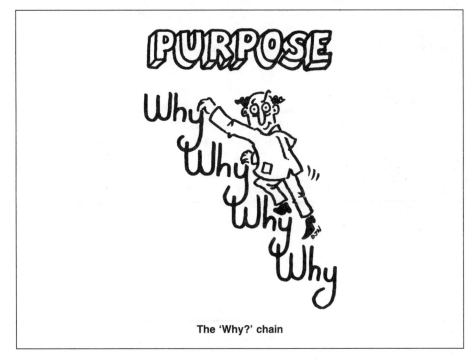

The 'Why?' chain

Exercise: Before you try the 'Why?' chain on your colleagues, apply it to yourself and your personal life. What are you trying to achieve in your personal life? Why? . . . Why? . . .

MARKET PERMIT EXPIRY

Each market grants an invisible or virtual permit to those with whom it wants to continue operating. Some products and services just do not get a permit in some markets. What does your permit say you can do?

If the market revoked your permit, what would you do?

1. Find another way of getting a permit (i.e., provide something else)?
2. Find another market that will issue a permit, and carry on providing the same thing?

If your answer was (1), what other products or services will you explore providing? Now stand back and look at the common elements. What are the common elements in those you used to provide and those you will start providing? That common element is your purpose.

If your answer was (2), what markets will you explore moving to? Now stand back and look at the common elements. What are both your previous market and your proposed markets buying? That common element is your purpose.

Exercise: Apply the market permit expiry tool to yourself before attacking your colleagues with it. Doing so will make you comfortable with the technique, and may turn out to be good contingency planning for your career!

WIPEOUT

Some alien race places your organisation inside a computer game. Along comes some nerd determined to make his or her day who wipes out your company with one push of a button. What crusade will have been ended? What journey that mankind ought to have been making will have been wiped out? What will the human race not have which it could have had without the wipeout? Assume you are the only people on earth capable of pursuing whatever it is, even though in reality many people and organisations can pursue the same purpose.

Exercise: If you were run over by a bus tomorrow, what purpose would be wiped out? Assume your purpose is unique.

TO MAKE ONE COMPANY, JUST ADD WATER

It had to happen eventually: 'instant company'. Get one at your supermarket today! Needless to say, there is a full product range, designed to suit every taste. Each is labelled with a company purpose.

Choose five from the selection of thousands. Name each one of your five instant companies as it appears on the product label.

When you get to the check-out desk, you find that you have left your instant share issue card at home. Damn! But you do have enough loose-change powder on you and just enough water in your flask (everyone carries one in a just-add-water society) to buy one? Which one will it be?

Exercise: Apply the same to your life. Choose five instant purposes, and then narrow it down to one.

Purpose is not created; it is discovered. It is not designed; it is distilled.

Once uncovered or distilled, it must be communicated if the knowledge of it is to have any use.

THE PURPOSE–VALUES LINK

Purpose and values are strongly linked. You are pursuing your purpose in a way that adheres to your values. Or put another way, your values give you guidelines with which to pursue your purpose. Can you see now why it is beneficial to separate them? Can you see now why we jump up and down when people confuse them? Can you see how they can give incredibly clear guidance to everyone in an organisation when they are making decisions, particularly to the directors and senior managers?

It is more important for a company to know what it is than where it is going. If it knows what it is *and* that it is going somewhere truly exciting, it is destined to be one of the best companies in economic history.

Strong values and an awesome purpose navigate companies into the future like an eternally burning beacon.

Constancy of, and conviction in values and purpose give anyone blessed with them more power than all of those who lack them.

IDENTIFYING YOUR VALUES

Values: the core beliefs an organisation holds and is not prepared to compromise under any circumstances.

WHAT VALUES DO, AND HOW

Shared values create self-control. The more strongly held the values are, the more self-directed, the more self-controlling, the more self-motivated the behaviour towards the end goal. The actual choice of values seems secondary to the fact that an organisation holds them and communicates them to all of the staff.

Much of this advice will horrify those who believe that the best way to run a business is to design systems so simple and thorough that even a trained monkey could produce the deliverables in that part of the business. That is a smart and sensible way to run a business. It means that you can employ lower-skilled workers than would be the case if no system existed and staff had to make all the decisions for themselves each time a deliverable was produced.

But no structured control system, no matter how rigorous, can cover every eventuality. That means that from time to time, people have to make their own decisions. If they have a strong set of values and a clear goal for their level of operation, they will be able to make those decisions.

Value-based control systems work because everyone at every 'deliverables point' has a clear means by which to make decisions. Fear-motivated control systems fail because they encourage the avoidance of risk-taking, they discourage initiative, and positively encourage doing only enough to get by.

Even the most fanatical control freaks cannot hope to control every action in any organisation of any size. Neither could they hope to know what the knock-on effects of any and every decision will be somewhere down the hierarchy. But the most liberal individual with a good understanding of culture can espouse a set of values, set up systems and make decisions that reflect those values and find themselves very quickly in an organisation where everyone controls themselves by reference to the values shared.

Exercise: If you still don't believe that values and purpose are the guidelines we use to make decisions at the highest level, what do you think we use?

THE POOR STATE OF THE STATUS QUO

How does culture reproduce itself in organisations which have yet to articulate a clear set of values? Partly through committees. Decisions are made in committees, where the long hours of debate eventually throw out a decision. The committee is utterly unaware that what was really going on in the confusion was that a decision was being made in the absence of values, in the absence of shared benchmarks against which the right or wrong decisions could be compared. Result: hours of debate to distil the norms (values, memes) that on this occasion are unknowingly agreed as the decision benchmark. Are the committees ever aware of the values behind each decision? Do they ever articulate or document the values with which the debate ended up agreeing? No. The decision is articulated and minuted, but the most useful thing – the value – is not. What happens? The next time a tough decision needs to be taken, the debates start all over again. And on goes the cycle of unproductivity.

Exercise: Think of the last time you had a long meeting or protracted debate over some small decision. What were the values being espoused on each side of the debate? When the debate was resolved, were the values that won the debate ever articulated? Were they documented? How long will it be before you are in the same meeting with the same people having the same debate over another issue?

THE RICH STATUS QUO

How does the above compare with what goes on in the best-aligned companies in the world? Their values are clearly spelled out. Their vision, mission, strategy, and so on are all clearly articulated. So when tough decisions have to be made, there is a clear and shared framework within which to make them. Needless to say, that removes the need for hours of heated norm-forming or value-eliciting debate.

Not all successful companies articulate their values; some symbolise them. That can be just as effective, or even more so, as long as you use symbols which are highly representative of the values you are seeking to communicate. For instance, Nike have their premises covered in pictures of high-achieving sports people from a wide range of sporting disciplines; Christians all over the world use the crucifix as a symbol of their values. I challenge you to find any sizeable organisation which does not symbolise what it stands for in some way.

Exercise: What are the five largest organisations with which you have dealings (professional and personal)? What symbols do they use?

IDENTIFYING WHAT VALUES ARE CURRENTLY IN PLACE

Values can be inferred from what your staff take pride in. They can be inferred by examining what you collectively perceive to be your core competence. They can be inferred from the way you add value to whatever it is you deliver (note the twin meaning of 'value' – it is yet another reason people get so confused about culture). For example, as a funeral director you 'add value' by dignifying a person's death for the benefit of their friends and family. You 'add value' by providing support and compassion. Would you go into the funeral business if you did not hold the values of dignity in death, supporting and compassion? Of course not.

Let's look at some tools for eliciting values.

Sentence-completion

Complete the following sentences with the first thing that comes to mind. Do not think about which answer to provide. Get an answer down as quickly as possible. We are trying to uncover your strongest values, the ones which are so deeply ingrained that they don't need any thought.

- We will . . .
- We agree to . . .
- We want to reflect . . .
- We want . . .
- We stand for . . .
- Our clients describe us as . . .
- Our competitors describe us as . . .
- Our suppliers describe us as . . .
- Our staff describe us as . . .
- Behaviour we find unacceptable is . . .

- The last thing we want to be is ...
- I would leave this company if it became ...
- I would go to work for another company if it was more ...

COMMON PROBLEMS IN IDENTIFYING CORE VALUES

Many of the answers to the above sentence-completion questions may not be values. Check your responses against all the definitions for the elements of the CAM. You will find a mixture of them all.

It was important that you appreciated that at first hand, so you could acknowledge the difficulty which others face when trying to give you their values. What we need are a range of tools to distil values and to distinguish values from behaviours, values from tactics, values from strategy and values from operating principles. Part of the difficulty comes from the fact that, more often than not, they overlap. Since values are the highest-order guidelines, you would expect to find their influence at all levels of a hierarchy.

Comparing ideal with actual

Establish the ideal of the culture. Seek such information from someone whose clear interest is to present the organisation in its best possible light. You are trying to determine the cultural ideal. Who has the strongest interest in presenting the rosiest picture of the culture?

Establish what is actually happening in an organisation (behaviours, decisions, systems as they actually happen, and so on) from people who have no interest in presenting the organisation in its best light. Often the people who really know what is actually going on are those who are least asked for their opinions: receptionists, secretaries, security staff, cleaners, people who are in lowly positions but who none the less speak to a large number of people, or who are in a position to overhear or oversee information.

Exercise: Name those people in your organisation.

Establish the gap between the idealised version of the culture the company would like to present and what is actually going on. Establish provisional lists of two sets of values: those espoused and those in use. The less aligned your culture, the greater will be the difference between the two sets.

Test your two lists by asking various 'deciders' about the bases for the decisions that have been made. Ask those observing or affected by the decisions what values they think were behind the decisions. If your hypotheses are right, you will find that those who make decisions espouse the idealised values, and everybody observes the decisions pointing to the 'values in use' list.

Exercise: Name five significant decisions you have witnessed in your career that were at odds with what the senior people making those decisions claimed was happening. What was your reaction in each case? Which set of values did you copy from then on?

COMPANY ENTRY

Throughout history in relatively free countries, the best people in any organisation have always been volunteers. Why? Well, they have the talents to do many other things with their lives. They can choose what to do and who to do it with. With such choice, those people will normally choose to work in fields and in organisations that have values compatible with their own. The chances are that since you are reading this book, you are one such talented volunteer. Why did you take one step forward for your current company? What is/are the value(s) you share? What, if it was changed, would mean that you would want to leave? What do your recruiters say about the company to attract talented people?

'I QUIT'

Drawing on your past experience, what are the top three things that would make you:

- leave the company?
- report a colleague?
- end an intimate relationship?
- end a friendship relationship?
- leave your religious grouping?

Exercise: Use your past experience to help you answer the questions. What negative aspects made you want to leave your last company? What made you end the last intimate relationship you ended? What made you walk away from the last friendship you felt you had to terminate?

FAMILY BREAK-UP

Which of your values are so important to you that, faced with the choice of your family breaking up or you sacrificing your values, you would rather minimise the pain of breaking up than lose your values? If you share your values with your family, you probably cannot imagine any circumstances in which this scenario could happen. If you have had a painful divorce, you probably cannot believe the naivety of those who cannot imagine this scenario. If you are in the latter category, what were the values that were at the centre of the divorce (nearly all divorces are about incompatible values).

COUNTRY EXIT

What values do you hold so dearly that if a new government denigrated and institutionalised the lower status of that value, you would leave your country? Those who value freedom have flocked to the USA for over two centuries. That means they are prepared to leave the countries of their birth for that value. What would make you leave your country? If the answer is 'nothing', your highest value is either patriotism or locational loyalty.

MYTHS: A CULTURE SNAPSHOT

Find out what stories and myths are regularly told. Find out who is regarded as a heroic figure. They usually embody the values in use in an organisation. What stories do those in charge of the induction programme tell? Who are the storytellers in your organisation? What stories do they tell of the organisation?

The epitomiser

Who would you send to an overseas conference to represent your company if a conference was called to document all the corporate cultures in the world, it was mandatory, and there were devastatingly heavy fines if you engaged in any misrepresentation? Who would epitomise your company, and why?

Drop it

If the markets you currently serve ceased to want something that represented a fundamental value to you, would you change your values or change your markets?

If a fundamental value, when manifested, put you at a competitive disadvantage in your current markets, would you drop the value or drop the market?

Let's wipe it out!

Propose to your team that you wipe out the organisation and all trace that it ever existed. Each member will be allocated an equally well paid job of the same type in other organisations, but everything else will go. Why would you not want that to happen? What is it about the organisation that makes it worth preserving? What does it represent that is worth keeping? What laudable value does it embody that would make you fight to preserve it?

Exercise: If you have ever left an organisation for entirely negative reasons, why would you be pleased to see that organisation wiped out? What negative value does it embody for you? The opposite of that value is probably close to the top of your value hierarchy.

Greenfield site

You are empowered to set up your own dream organisation. Leaving aside what it does, what will be its values? Pull together a draft list of values

Many of the things you uncover in your search for the fundamental values of the organisation may not make the sacred list of values. Many such things may make it onto the tactics, strategies, operating principles or other lists: be sure to distinguish between them.

PRIORITISING THE VALUES

Choice methods: ranking

Having collected a range of contender values in your attempt to establish the most widely held values in the organisation, the task now is to find out which are the most important, which ones are used in decision-making processes.

Present a list of values, and ask the person(s) whose values you are trying to elicit to rank their top ten. Present a series of values in pairs and ask which is held most highly.

Forced choice   When you have identified a number of contender values, pair each with every other and ask for a priority ranking. Collate all the answers from each team member to arrive at the highest-held values of the group.

Dilemma-distilling   Present a series of everyday dilemmas and ask for decisions. The decisions will be very revealing and enable you to distil the underlying values. If you want the values to be more business-focused, make all the dilemmas business dilemmas. For example, one of your staff has blatantly disobeyed one of your explicit directives in front of your entire department, after having been warned not to. But there's one catch: the result of their disobedience is the one result you have been pushing towards for the last few months. What do you do: reprimand or dismiss, on the grounds that disobeying directives is not to be tolerated whatever the outcome, or praise and reward the individual for having the good judgement to know when to disobey directives?

You are keen on health and fitness and language-learning. A situation arises where you are faced with a choice of either going to the gymnasium or your language class, but you can't do both. What would you do: go to the gym, or go to the language class? The answer gives an indication of whether you value health above language-learning, or vice versa

The answer to those and other dilemmas will enable you and your staff to rank your values.

Exercise: Compile a list of such dilemmas. Pit one value against another, and ask the people whose values you are seeking to uncover to resolve the dilemmas. Try to base the dilemmas on real-life decisions which most people are likely to have faced. Try to base the dilemmas on the values you think the company may hold.

DECIDING WHAT VALUES TO FORMALLY ADOPT

Now you have identified and prioritised the values the organisation actually holds, you are immediately faced with a dilemma. Do you formally adopt the values which you have established are most prevalent in the organisation, or do you adopt the values which, although not most prevalent, are sufficiently in evidence for them to be credible adoptees?

Do you formally adopt values actually in use which may reflect the worst in human nature (greed, deceit, apathy or worse), on the grounds that culture change only works if it is close to the existing culture, or do you adopt the values espoused, suspecting that they will be swamped by the more widely practised values in use?

Not an easy call. Some organisations are so steeped in values which epitomise the worst in human nature that the best thing for everyone would be to shut down and start again from a greenfield site. But given commercial realities, you as CEO don't really have that option, do you? So what do you do? Remember that people will go to extraordinary lengths to live and realise values they truly hold, values that epitomise the noble spirit. Well, take the values of that type you have identified in the organisation as being most prevalent, and formally adopt them. But before you do, there are a few things you need to check to ensure the proposed values are OK.

VALUE MATCHES: VALUES AND STAKEHOLDERS

Check your draft list of values against this list of major stakeholders. Do they hold your proposed values? If they do not, are the proposed values near the top of their value hierarchy?

- Customers
- Employees
- Suppliers
- Humanity/community
- Ourselves

If a company holds a value which will alienate one of its stakeholder groups, it is headed for trouble: not for holding the value *per se*, but for the behaviour which will ultimately manifest from those values.

VALUE–PURPOSE MATCH

Having established your values, or decided which you wish to move towards, go back to your purpose and establish how they are compatible. If your purpose is to provide dignity in death and you value enthusiasm and rapid change, you might have a bit of a problem. If there is a mismatch, it is likely something has gone wrong in the process of uncovering values or purpose. Draw the attention of your team to the mismatch, and seek to uncover the values that would have led you to the purpose distilled. Or seek to uncover the purpose which logically ought to have emerged from the values identified.

PUTTING THE ADOPTED VALUES IN PLACE

Having established that the proposed values satisfy your checks, you are now in the position of having to put in place everything that is necessary for those values to be manifested as actual behaviour. Let's look at how to achieve that.

REWARDS AND VALUES

Successful culture change or alignment is never instant. It is rarely quick. It is always achieved by example. It must be achieved by setting up a cascade. Decisions you make about what to reward and what to penalise in your subordinates will have a direct effect on their behaviour. That will affect the decisions they make about their charges. This will, in turn, affect their subordinates' behaviour. Culture change is usually a cascade of decisions and behaviour.

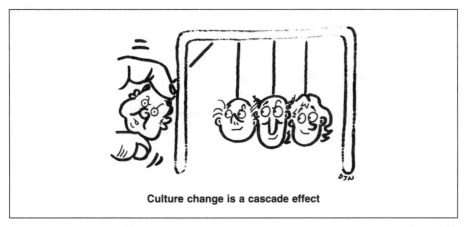

Culture change is a cascade effect

People adopt the values and beliefs which bring them advantage. People will change their beliefs if it is in their long-term best interests to do so. How do they determine whether their best interests are served? By assessing whether or not they are rewarded by holding their current beliefs; by noting what their superiors believe. People instinctively know that they will be rewarded for believing or appearing to believe what their superiors believe. Whatever you hold as values or beliefs will determine what you reward, and how. If you want to change or align your culture, you must reward that which you want, and penalise (or ignore) that which you don't.

Exercise: Have a look at your current reward system. What values are being rewarded? Are they those you wish to encourage?

VALUES AND BEHAVIOURS

Implementing the CAM and achieving any culture change is more about getting behaviour change than getting values to change. Directors at ASDA, the UK supermarket chain, changed the culture to one of service (internally and externally oriented) partly by having staff wear badges with their first name and a statement committing them to be 'happy to help'. It proved to be a constant, effective reminder of the desired new culture.

Behaviour-induced value change

If you have good reason to suspect that people will not change their values easily, try counter-attitudinal advocacy. This phenomenon leads people to change their values towards matching their behaviour. That is, if people are motivated to behave ethically by rewards for doing so, they will be more likely to hold ethical values after such behaviour than before. In change terms: make rewards lead behaviour, and behaviour leads values. If you want to change values, change rewards. Once the new behaviours have been in place for a few months (that's all it takes), follow by formally documenting the new values.

Understanding why values are held, and changing them

What will encourage people to buy into a set of values they do not currently hold? First, we ought to say that getting people to agree with values that are the exact opposite of those they currently hold is neither easy nor quick. It can be done, but the cost of doing so is much greater than finding those who already and naturally share your values. Second, we should say that it is probably worth working only on those who have values close to those you wish to be the shared values (refer to *Counselling for Managers*, MacLennan 1996, for much more on changing beliefs and values).

Exercise: Who were the last five people you had to dismiss? Why did they have to go? What did they do or not do? What values did their behaviour clash with?

VALUES AND RECRUITMENT

What is going on in an interview? Is it checking that the shortlisted candidates can do the job? No. Probably 40 per cent of all applicants can do the job, and certainly 100 per cent of the people at the shortlist stage can do the job. It is obviously nothing to do with whether the person can do the job or not. So what is the interview about? It is a values compatibility check. Well, in the best companies it is. (Given that all shortlisted candidates are known to be able to do the job, why do companies bother with psychometric testing?)

But since most companies haven't spelled out their values, how can they carry out the check? They can't! Well at least not very well, and certainly not as well as they could if the values were clearly articulated.

Exercise: How do you currently check for a values match at interviews?

Strong values attract the strong and feed their strengths.

If people do not buy into the organisation's values, they have to go. Remove them if after repeated explanations of the values and their importance they consistently behave in ways inconsistent with the shared values.

CHECKING THAT THE VALUES HAVE BEEN ADOPTED

WHAT EVIDENCE?

Taking the list of contender values you wish the company to stand for, ask what evidence tells you that each value is being met. What evidence would tell you each particular value is not being met? That starts to tell you what behaviours you can expect to see in the company once the values are widely communicated, shared and adopted. Some examples are given below.

Nearly there, but still getting it wrong

One major organisation (their name will not be revealed – all negative case histories in this book which go into detail are anonymous) I know of has five stated values:

1. empowerment and support for high expectations
2. people as individuals
3. families and communities
4. straight forward and better
5. ambassadors for communication

This company has stated publicly that it does not and will not be making the value list known to its staff. It claims to have appointed a champion at director level to promote the adoption and practice of the values. It claims that the values are practised on a day-to-day basis. What do you think? Can you imagine a scenario where directors know the company's values, but the staff do not? Unlikely. Can you imagine a scenario in which someone is championing a value without revealing what that value is? Unlikely. Can you imagine that publishing this information in a national journal (as it was) is not going to mean that the staff get hold of it? Unlikely. Can you imagine that publicly telling staff that you will not be telling staff what the values are while at the same time documenting them for everyone to see in a public source is going to have anything other than a negative effect on staff perceptions of the management? Unlikely.

Another company, a major banking establishment in the UK, claims to have a shared set of values, but won't chronicle them. Again this information was volunteered to an influential national business journal. What conclusions would you draw from that if you were a staff member, a supplier, a customer or an investor?

PRACTISE WHAT YOU PREACH

Any espousal of values, to be credible, needs to be perpetually and repeatedly consummated by actions and decisions.

For values to be adopted, they must be practised as they are preached. A major subsidiary of one of the world's largest companies has this as one of its values:

'resource conservation and energy efficiency'. Nothing wrong with that, you might say. That is until you notice that the values statement, vision and a few international awards are each proudly displayed and mounted in very expensive brass frames. Above each is a designer brass picture light expensively shining a high-powered spotlight onto the frame. All that in an exceptionally well-lit room with high ceilings and huge, single-glazed windows.

Now how seriously would you take that company's value statements? Would you believe they were serious about resource conservation and energy efficiency? Or would you draw conclusions about the sincerity of the organisation and make assumptions about how wide the gap was between word and deed in other aspects of the company's conduct?

Exercise: What behaviours would you expect to see from such a value? What behaviours would you definitely not expect to see?

When espoused and evident values are different, the former are ignored and the latter are copied.

Successful change is about hundreds of people implementing thousands of changes using one single and simple guiding framework.

Staff and managers not prepared to behave in ways consistent with the desired new culture are first trained, then enticed, and finally terminated. They are replaced by those who epitomise the new culture.

ESTABLISHING SHARED VALUES BY EXAMPLE

Forrest Mars (the founder of Mars) established the company's number one value and reinforced it with the motto: 'I want to be proud of our products.'

We have already said that the best way to disseminate values is by example and by rewarding people for behaving in ways consistent with those values.

Mars's staff developed a new product. On tasting it, Mars noticed differences which he identified as being related to lower-quality ingredients. He immediately called a meeting of directors and the others involved in this new product. He asked them to taste the product. The difference was very noticeable. The product was never put out for market testing.

The key point here is that instead of just making a decision and enforcing it, he used the tasting event to demonstrate what happened when low-quality materials were used. The result of that example – everyone could see that quality genuinely came first, and agreed that it should. Quality is still a central value in the company today.

Values are established and maintained by example, by actual practice. Words rarely, if ever, establish values.

Exercise: What examples of living the values have your company leaders recently set?

Marks & Spencer place a similar importance on quality. The directors and managers literally live, eat and sleep their products. They wear them, they eat them, they decorate their houses with them. Why? Quality assurance. If you as a senior manager don't want to use it, whatever it is, what makes you think that your customers will be prepared to use it? That is one sure way to make sure an organisation provides quality *and* shows all the staff that quality really is valued.

GETTING IT RIGHT . . . OR NEARLY RIGHT

General Electric are. Their CEO, Jack Welsh, established a culture that should see GE able to cope with the best competition for up to twenty years. Of course, it will need to be tweaked and tuned on an ongoing basis. It follows all the rules for an effective culture. There are three main values:

- boundarylessness
- stretch
- speed

Boundarylessness

People all over the world complain that demarcation lines and functional divisions in their companies slow down their work, and usually create more work than they are supposed to save. In valuing boundarylessness, GE are acknowledging that frustration, and are holding a value which will result in behaviours and working practices that will enable staff to do their jobs better.

Stretch

We all know that incremental goals don't inspire. A percentage point on the profit margin here and a part per thousand improvement on the quality standard there just don't get people excited. Stretch is about valuing challenge, it is about giving people something that is going to switch them on, body, mind and soul. Good stretch goals go beyond that which you could conceive of achieving even in a best-case scenario.

Speed

Speed of response impresses customers everywhere. When you value speed over, say, authority, you see less petty politicking. You see people doing those things that will produce results quickest, in preference to bickering over who has control over which members of staff.

Exercise: What behaviours, policies and reward systems would you expect to see in place from GE's values?

Exercise: The title to this section, 'Getting it right . . . or nearly right', alluded to a suggestion that GE's values don't quite fit the bill. Which one of them do you think is something else masquerading as a value? What is that something else?

SUMMARY

The best-aligned companies in the world have clearly articulated values, and those values guide the behaviour and decision-making of the people in them.

If you are to align your culture, you first need to know what the values of the culture actually are, not just what your PR people might try to claim they are. Then you, and your staff, must decide what values you collectively want to live by. You should take that draft list and compare it to the values of the major stakeholder groups. Assuming everything matches well, you then have to put in place the systems and structures which will reward behaviour based on those values. Finally, you will have to devise a range of measures to determine if the desired culture is in place in the way you envisaged.

7 Forming an awesome purpose, vision and mission

CHAPTER OVERVIEW

- The status quo
- The benefits of awesome purpose, vision and mission
- Defining awesome purpose
- Where does awesome purpose fit in the CAM?
- Beyond mission and objectives
- Breaking the rules successfully
- Creating a vision/mission/awesome purpose
- Testing the awesome purpose
- Awesome purposes and experimentation
- Assumption checks
- Summary

In this chapter we will consider how to arrive at a vision, mission or awesome purpose. They are being considered together because although they are brought into existence for different reasons and at different times, they are arrived at by the same route.

To remind you: a vision is the longest-term end point you set in pursuit of your purpose (8–25 years), a mission is the mid-term end point (3–8 years), and the awesome purpose brings together most or all of the elements of the CAM in a highly inspiring way.

Now let us explore the background to vision, mission and awesome purpose, and how to form them.

THE STATUS QUO

Most companies have no vision or mission. Most organisations' mission state-ments (if they have one – most don't; 98 per cent of all businesses don't even have a business plan!) are a hotchpotch of vague aspirations, platitudes, norms, practices, tactics, methods, product statements, and worse.

Most companies have no vision

Exercise: What are your company's mission and vision? Can you quote them word for word, without looking them up?

The most common type of flawed vision/mission statement is the platitude. Like 'motherhood and apple pie', most platitudes are so generalised as to be meaningless.

Is a dismal mission statement worse than none at all? Yes. The reason for having a mission statement (and all the elements discussed here) is to give staff a means of making decisions; it is to give those who have been empowered a basis for making decisions; it is to remove the need for stifling command and control structures. A poor mission statement (one which is unclear, difficult to remember or too complex to decipher) does not give guidance. Put that in place and loosen the command and control structure, and what happens? Staff lose their bearings. There is no basis to make decisions. The thing they used to depend on has gone, and the new tool is useless.

INVISIBLE MISSION STATEMENTS

Lack of a mission statement or lack of a clear mission statement does not necessarily mean there is no mission in an organisation. Many workplaces buzz with a sense of shared vision or mission, but nowhere is it written down. Or if it is written down, it is not done well. One of the most successful companies in the world has an unbelievably poor mission statement. It rambles on for weeks. But the reports which regularly come out of the company are consistent in saying there is a very strong sense of mission.

Exercise: Have you ever worked in an organisation where there was no documented mission yet there was a strong sense of mission? How was that sense of mission created?

In such places, the mission is conveyed by speech and interaction. Some companies will be tempted to say: 'Oh yes, that's us. Yes, we have a sense of mission. We don't have to worry about articulating it.' If you are a Sony, you can get away with it for a while, as long as the powerful vision painted by the dynamic founder of the organisation is still visible. Even that will fade, and it will have to be replaced. Most companies do not have a mission, not even one conveyed verbally. However, most, if not all companies like to kid themselves that they do.

But that does not mean that a good vision does not exist somewhere in the organisation. Take a look at your consistently highest-performing managers, as long as you can be sure that their performance is not a function of them just happening to be in the most lucrative market. Find out what their operating vision is. If their staff are performing at extraordinary levels, you can be sure that behind that performance there will be some vision that most or all of them buy into.

As with values, it is more important that an organisation has a mission or vision than what the mission statement is. But many I see are so long and confusing that they could only be described by their authors as 'mission statements'. Some are so bad that they signal to one and all that the organisation has no mission. 'Short on mission, soporifically long on platitudes' was the phrase used to describe one company's mission when I was conducting the final research for this book.

THE BENEFITS OF AWESOME PURPOSE, VISION AND MISSION

If you have 50, 500, 5 000 or 50 000 people in your organisation, you have that number of perceptions of reality. The same applies to the perception of your vision or awesome purpose. Even if it is wonderfully inspiring and follows all the guidelines which we are about to lay down, each of your staff will see it slightly differently. But, having established a shared vision, you will have much more alignment than those companies with a weak or confusing mission, and much, much more alignment than those with no vision at all.

Do you navigate your future by looking over your shoulder to study the contours of your footsteps? So why do most companies insist on plotting their future by reading their accounts? Why do they try and navigate into the future using an accounting map which is out of date before the first figures are gathered, rather than deciding what future they want to create and drawing their own map. In other words, why do businesses plan using out-of-date information? Bizarre.

Exercise: Does your company plan its future by looking at last year's accounts? Before you answer, perhaps you should ask this question: 'How does my company plan its future?'

FUTURE-FORMING

What is the most important aspect of thinking about the future? Understanding the principles that drive the people who create a business. To paraphrase Henry Ford: 'The deeper the understanding of the foundations (principles) of any subject you have attained, the higher you will be able build your future.'

An awesome purpose is about envisioning a future, then creating it. If your draft awesome purpose does not frighten you and send shivers up your spine, it probably won't be a hit with your staff either. Awesome purposes create the future by providing an inspiring expectation of the future. Companies which have them create the future by drawing a map of it, and then use that map to navigate to the pinnacle of that industry. For them, the future is not something to be arrived at. It is to be created.

An awesome purpose should be based on virtually unreasonable confidence and require superhuman commitment. It should transcend its author; any one person in the company, indeed it should transcend the company itself. It should be something that represents a human advance. Such an advance may be providing something many people want at a price few people can believe, or providing something so quickly that customers think the company providing it must be psychic, or providing something that performs so well that it defies explanation by the non-expert. That takes us to the link between awesome purpose and strategy (there is more on strategy-formation on pages 104–130).

Exercise: What is your greatest achievement? When you were striving towards it, how did you represent it to yourself? What picture of it did you hold in your mind? What got you charged up about it?

DEFINING AWESOME PURPOSE

ARE WE GOOD ENOUGH?

An awesome purpose should be tough, with a possibility that it might not be achieved. It should be achievable, but the question in people's minds should be: 'Is it achievable by us?'

MAKE IT UNDERSTANDABLE

An awesome purpose must be simple, because it must be understood by all your stakeholders. It should involve simple and few words. (Volvo chose 'safety'.)

MAKE IT NEW AND EXCITING

An awesome purpose should be attempting something new and exciting, something that has not been done before. It should rule out everything but what it seeks to go for.

IGNORE PART OF YOUR MARKET

Volvo are not seeking to capture the sexy sports car market. They walk away from that market. If your awesome purpose does not require you to walk away from a segment of your market, it is not an awesome purpose.

PURPOSE IS NOT VISION

Neither is an awesome purpose the kind of contortion many companies create in order to embrace everything they do. For instance, British Telecom is not a communications company, it is a telecommunications company. If you are looking for a phrase that embraces everything you do, you will not inspire, you will merely tell people what they already know in a tight little phrase. There may be some use for that, but it is not establishing an awesome purpose.

THE BUSINESS YOU ARE IN IS NOT AN AWESOME PURPOSE

Most businesses struggle to answer the question 'What business are we in?' or the components of it, as we saw earlier. But answering that question is not generating an awesome purpose. Yes, you need to know your purpose and direction. Yes, identifying your purpose and direction are necessary steps in formulating an awesome purpose. But they are not an awesome purpose. As a business author, amongst other things, I can shout 'I'm in the communications business' until I'm blue in the face, but it won't make 'I'm in the communications business' an awesome purpose, will it?

MEANING

Most people are desperate to have some meaning in their lives. As monotheistic religious belief continues to decline more and more, people are left with a sense of purposelessness. People want to feel meaning in their lives. If you can give your staff a strong and worthwhile sense of purpose, if you can give their lives some meaning, if you can give them a wonderful goal to pursue, they will pour in all of their creative talents and energies and be pleased to contribute. Give them an awesome purpose, and your staff will give you awesome performance.

INSPIRING LANGUAGE

If you think I'm using excessively flowery and rhetorical language to make these points, you just have not got it. Look at all the examples of awesome purposes in the book. Are they expressed in bland and dull language? Most definitely not. To provide an awesome purpose, you must, absolutely *must* make it as vivid and real in the minds of others as possible. If people can't imagine what they are working towards, there is little chance they will get excited about it.

Getting them to imagine it is the first step. Getting them to imagine it and feel the emotional impact that the achievement will have is the second. Using emotionally laden language is almost essential, if not in the awesome purpose statement itself then certainly in the supporting speeches and documentation. Did Churchill say 'Now look here chaps, we need to teach these naughty Nazis a lesson'? No. He used the full command of his incredible linguistic skills, fine-tuned over many years of book-writing and public speaking, to empassion the world to unite and defend the causes of freedom and democracy against darkness and tyranny.

'LET ME AT THE COMPETITION!'

People want to compete, and doubly so when they believe they can win, when they believe they have a winning vision. People all over the world claim to be and think of themselves as the best in their fields. Harness the desire to prove that. Give them a vision, mission or awesome purpose which, if achieved, would deem them indisputably the best. Remember Komatsu's awesome purpose: 'to encircle Caterpillar' (their biggest competitor).

Exercise: What meaning does your current company provide for its staff? If the current focus (vision, mission, awesome purpose) holds no meaning, rewrite it so that it does hold meaning. What cause does it fight for? How can your staff prove they are the best?

WILLING TO MARCH INTO HELL FOR A HEAVENLY CAUSE

People all over the world seek to do that which is right and just. The social evolution of the human race is the history of the battles between those seeking to do what is right and those seeking to protect their self-interest. Those seeking right may lose individual battles, but decade after decade, century after century, they win the wars of their time, and will continue to do so. Give your people a just cause to fight for, and watch their performance levels.

An awesome purpose provides a measure against which you can assess if your staff are headed in the right direction.

PRETTY PICTURES

An awesome purpose paints a picture. It contains something people can see: 'a man on the moon'. It is an easy-to-imagine and remember picture of an end point. An awesome purpose has picturable outcomes.

Exercise: What picture does your company paint of the end point you are striving towards (if, that is, any end point has been articulated)?

SUMMARY: DEFINING VISIONS, MISSIONS, AWESOME PURPOSES

We have talked about what awesome purposes must do and look like at some length, so let's pull together everything stated and implied into a few checklists.

Awesome purposes:

- must be clear
- must be simple
- must be focused
- must be exclusive
- should be spine-tingling
- contain an end point (output/product/process)
- contain an end point image
- may provide an enemy
- should be unifying
- must be future-creating

A good vision, mission and awesome purpose must be:

- communicable
- coherent
- comprehensible
- captivating
- communicated

Other factors that define an awesome purpose, vision and mission:

- applicable
- inspiring
- memorable

To make it memorable, it must be both distinctive and simple. KISS: Keep It Simple, Stupid. The shorter and clearer it is, the better.

Applicable

People must feel that the awesome purpose applies to them. They must be able to see how they can contribute. All groups of stakeholders must feel that it is applicable to them. Obviously, any awesome purpose must be more applicable to some stakeholder groups than others. The two most important groups to satisfy are the customers and the staff. The staff are trying to achieve something awesome for the customers (and all of humanity). Satisfy those groups, and all others will usually have their needs met: shareholders will (capital growth), suppliers will (more business with you), the community will (more jobs and disposable income in the local community).

An awesome purpose must be central to customer needs and/or customer problems and/or aspirations, either directly or indirectly. If the customer does not see that your awesome purpose is applicable to them, they probably won't buy whatever awesome benefit you are seeking to provide.

Inspiring

If a vision is not in the hearts of your people, it is nowhere. If your vision does not fire your people, your people will fire you. They will go where their passion is wanted; where they can be all they can be; where they are inspired.

Memorable

An awesome purpose is heard once and never forgotten. For example:

> Put a man on the moon.

> Government of the people, by the people, for the people.

> A Coke™ within arm's reach of everyone on the planet.

You will see plenty more examples peppered throughout the book.

WHERE DOES AN AWESOME PURPOSE FIT IN THE CAM?

It is an all-encompassing expression of where the organisation is going, why, and how. An awesome purpose summarises the CAM; it embraces most or all of the CAM. As such, there will be flavours of each element of the CAM in the awesome purpose.

Yet the awesome purpose is inevitably more strongly associated with some parts of the CAM than others. The following positions give a guide to the parts of the CAM an awesome purpose usually draws most heavily from:

- Values
- Purpose (C)
- Direction
- Vision (A)
- Mission (A)
- Strategy
- Major objectives (B)
- Tactics
- Objectives
- Operating principles

(A) is an ideal position for an awesome purpose. (B) is an acceptable position for an awesome purpose. (C) is an acceptable but rare position for an awesome purpose.

Awesome purposes can be set at any of the three points where targets are set, and to a lesser extent at the Purpose level. Having said that, your awesome purpose, although it must be phrased as an end point, could be drawn from virtually any level in the CAM.

Awesome purposes, from whichever level they draw most heavily, must be interpretable at the operational level. Those charged with delivering each of the deliverables in the CAM must be able to interpret the awesome purpose and use it for guidance in their roles.

BEYOND MISSION AND OBJECTIVES

Note that a major benefit of the Corporate Alignment Model is made clear here: we've moved from mere goal-setting (management by objectives and mission statements) to establishing goals of different magnitude against a higher-order framework. Not that this is new. The words have been in our language for a long time. Neither is this any great discovery; it is simply a collection of observations pulled together from some of the best companies in the world.

The Corporate Alignment Model is just a handle to describe what the corporate alignment benchmark companies have been doing for some time. Indeed, the best leaders of all time, from the Founding Fathers of the USA to Alexander the Great, Napoleon through to Churchill would, we hope, see this model as one way of explaining what they did. And of course that's exactly what it is: the model is no more or less than their actions defined, ordered and systematised for all to understand and copy. Can you afford not to learn from people of that calibre? I can't.

Exercise: If you are not happy with the examples given or the conclusions drawn, I suggest you get hold of some good texts on leadership and research the techniques of great leaders for yourself (for example, *Effective Leadership*, Adair 1983; *Leaders on Leadership*, Crainer 1996).

BREAKING THE RULES SUCCESSFULLY

Some financial visions which under our rules should not work do work. ICI's Sir John Harvey-Jones set an awesome purpose: to be the first British industrial company to achieve a billion-pound profit. Why did that apparent breach of our awesome purpose rules work? Possibly because there was so much slack in the company that it was relatively easy to make savings that took the profit levels up. Much more likely is that the directors, senior managers and managers all knew that achieving that target would be good for their careers. Being responsible for a part of the first billion-pound company looks pretty good on a CV. So maybe we ought to qualify our awesome purpose rules.

Financial goals *may* work if they are sufficiently symbolic of something much, much more important. Alas, I've found that as soon as bead-counters hear the first part of that amendment (they are deaf to the second part), they jump to the conclusion that it's business as usual. 'Add 5 per cent to the profit target, that will get them going.' It won't. ICI's landmark was exceptional. In this instance, it is the exception that proves the rule.

CREATING A VISION/MISSION/AWESOME PURPOSE

Visions are more collated than created; more borrowed than built.

Visions, missions and awesome purposes are not created by writing fancy phrases on a piece of paper and distributing it. Visions are not created in the lead of pencils, but in the hearts of people.

How do you develop an awesome purpose? By going through the following three stages:

1. Refer to higher-level guidelines (Purpose, Values).
2. Collate and collect; distil and define; create and condense.
3. Test, test and test again.

Now let us look at some specific techniques to create a vision/mission/awesome purpose.

COMBINING INTERESTS

Vision statements and awesome purposes are arrived at slowly, gradually, by steeping yourself in the key customer and staff issues.

Creating an awesome purpose is about finding a link between what your customers want and what your staff want. Whatever you come up with must also satisfy the other stakeholder groups.

It is about satisfying the emotional needs of your people. Your people want to achieve something spectacular, to be involved in something bigger than themselves, to have a strong sense of meaning, passion and purpose. They want the way they spend their most productive years to amount to something. Can you imagine the pride those 100 000 or so people who were involved in the first moonshot must feel now? Many of them will be retired or nearing retirement. Can you imagine the sense of having made a contribution that they must feel?

It is about seeking views from your suppliers, from your backers, from your other stakeholder groups.

Achieving your vision can only be done by drawing on the aspirations of all stakeholder groups. Failing to do that will make your vision real in only one place: your mind.

An awesome purpose must be drawn from the needs and desires of all the stakeholders. It cannot be something concocted in a darkened room by a few dizzy academics with less than five seconds' real-life business experience between them. Companies that involve their stakeholders in the formation of a vision find strong levels of co-operation with the vision which emerges.

Exercise: What is the current process for generating your company's vision?

BENEFIT ELEMENTS

Describe the benefits you find exciting, and express them as an end point you also find exciting – as many as possible – then mould each into some short, sharp image. It *must* be based on commercial realities. That is not to say that an awesome purpose cannot have a spiritual, philosophical or messianic slant to it. It should have all of these things, but to be credible it must reach for the spiritual from a strong commercial foundation.

Exercise: Taking your greatest achievement from a previous exercise, what was the spiritual element to it?

Companies that set up systems and structures which make it possible for their staff to contribute ideas towards the realisation of the vision achieve their objectives faster than those who don't. You won't be surprised to find that many of the best-aligned companies in the world are also the most innovative.

Exercise: Why do you think that is so?

COLLECT OBJECTIVES AND MAJOR OBJECTIVES

You can pull together an awesome purpose by gathering all the operating objectives at the various levels in the organisation. Your better managers will have set inspiring goals for their teams. They may already have the awesome purpose you seek.

IF ONLY . . .

If you can make this company do one wonderful thing, anything you want, something that will take a few years, something that has never been done before or as well, what would it be?

YOU HAVE A DREAM

You can also start the search for an awesome purpose by starting a discussion amongst all the groups and committees in the organisation. Ask them for their dreams. Propose some draft visions, and ask them to improve them. Ask for inspiring versions of the goals; ask for other goals that might have the desired effect – a united and inspired workforce.

IT'S ABOUT INVOLVEMENT, IDIOT!

If you want your people to be passionately committed to any part of the CAM, which of the following do you think is preferable? Seek their views, collate them, feed them back for more, involve your people in the entire process, or you and the top team decide behind a closed door which of the boffins' recommendations to accept, and then impose it on the whole organisation. If the answer is not obvious, you had best put down this book, it has nothing more to offer you.

TESTING THE AWESOME PURPOSE

Test it on yourself and the others in the team charged with collating it first, using some acid-test questions, such as: 'What would you sacrifice or give up to achieve this goal?' (if it is not something of value to you, you don't have an awesome purpose); 'To what lengths are you prepared to go to achieve this goal?' (if you are not prepared to do something that really puts you out, you don't have an awesome purpose); 'If you could work for any other organisation, which one would it be? Why?' (if your answer is anything to do with them having an awesome purpose you believe in, you and your company have not found an awesome purpose that works for you).

TEST THE IMAGE–STATEMENT MATCH

What will the awesome purpose look like when you have achieved it? You may know what you want to be done, but do you have a clear way of expressing it? If you don't, then talk to your people, tell them what you want, and ask them how it should be expressed. Tell other people what it is, ask them what they think it will mean, what they think it is inviting them to do. If they then tell you what you had originally envisaged, then you've got it right. If not, back to the proverbial drawing board. Do it right there, right then. Ask them what they think would best express what you have in mind.

When you test your vision with your people, what effect does it have on them? Getting an honest verbal reaction can often be a problem. But it is much more difficult to please the boss with body language. What do they look like when they hear your draft vision? Do their eyes start to sparkle and dart around their heads as they see the range of possibilities? Or do they glaze over? Do they seem to grow in size, look taller, fill more volume? Or do they shrink and wither? Do they look a bit excited and a bit frightened? Or do they epitomise apathy? If you have an awesome purpose, you will see the positive reactions in the above contrasts.

If you get a good reaction over and over again as you test your draft awesome purpose, you have probably got an awesome purpose. The above process was exactly that which I followed when trying to come up with an appropriate label to describe the concept which ultimately was called 'awesome purpose'. Now, I meet people several years after a consultancy job or a workshop and the first thing they say beyond the brief hellos and pleasantries is 'awesome purpose'.

If you really have an awesome purpose statement, it will find its way round the company faster than any official announcements. You will hear people who never usually pay much attention to what is going on using the phrase and discussing it with their colleagues.

TESTING WHETHER THE AWESOME PURPOSE IS WORKING

If you have an awesome purpose, people will start changing little things about their jobs before the awesome purpose is properly in place. They will start taking initiatives where there was no history of such behaviour. They will start showing ownership of problems where they previously would have ignored them or passed them off as 'not part of my job'.

People will ask higher authorities for decisions less often. They will take decisions on their own, guided by the clarity of the vision.

Customers will start to notice the difference, and when they do complain about the inevitable mistakes, they will start making reference to the things going wrong not being in line with the stated vision.

You will see a reduced turnover of staff. People want to stay where their contribution to some lofty cause is welcome.

You will see an increase in the number and quality of applications for jobs. You will see a dramatic increase in unsolicited applications. You will notice reference to your awesome purpose in covering letters with applications.

Exercise: What other indicators would you expect which would tell you that your awesome purpose was having the desired effect?

MORE EXAMPLES OF THOSE GETTING IT RIGHT, OR ALMOST RIGHT

Let us take a walk through a few different industries and add to the already large number of awesome purposes.

Transport

One of the best examples of an awesome purpose being achieved is that of the New York City Transit Company. Infamous throughout the world, the system was even avoided by hardened New Yorkers. It was in terminal decline, crime-ridden, covered in graffiti, and an object of public ridicule. We know that where graffiti is tolerated, criminals take that as a signal that other crime will go undetected as well. So once the graffiti appears and nothing is done to stop it, any neighbourhood thus afflicted rapidly goes downhill. Even the residents seem to care less for an area when the rot has started.

Then in 1984 the awesome purpose 'No Graffiti' was set. If you never saw the New York underground in the state it was then, you may not appreciate just how awesome such a target was.

What's the situation now? New York has a model subway system. There is no graffiti. Crime has been reduced by 60 per cent of its previous level. Customer satisfaction went up 30 per cent. All this with 5 per cent fewer staff. If you have any friends in New York, phone them, ask them what the subway is like now compared to the late 1970s and early 1980s.

Finance

An awesome purpose must have deep meaning. It must capture the soul. Some cynical readers may say: 'It is OK going for deep spiritual meaning when you are defending democracy or sending man to the moon, but we are in the finance industry [or any industry you think might be difficult to spiritualise]; it can't be done.' It *can* be done. It has *been* done. It *continues* to be done.

> We are the custodians of our customers' financial dreams. (Charles Schwab, a large American financial organisation)

If you put soul into your business purpose, your staff will put their souls into the business. If you are on the ball, you will already be jumping up and down protesting that I have just presented what is very clearly a purpose statement. Yes it is, but it has been included because it is a rare example of a purpose statement which is also an awesome purpose.

Manufacturing

Mission and strategy are not fixed. Recently, Boeing changed its strategy (while sticking within the framework set by their purpose and values) to fast delivery at low cost, to reduce costs and time of manufacture in order to increase an already commanding lead. The major objectives coming from that are: 'Reduce the time to manufacture a plane from eighteen months to eight months in four years. Reduce costs by 25 per cent in six years.' Now, in terms of our definition, that is too numerical to be an awesome purpose, but like the ICI example, they are collectively such monstrous objectives that they get away with breaking the rules.

Numerically based awesome purposes are not ideal, but they can work well if they conjure up a highly specific picture. Here is one more example of that.

3M, probably the most prolifically innovative company in commercial history, have constant innovation (the development of new products to solve old problems) as their strategy. Their 'awesome purpose' is to generate 30 per cent of their revenues from products which did not exist four years ago. How does it work? Well, I cannot speak for others here, but the image it brings to mind is a line of people, a quarter of whom are newborn babies. What image does it bring to mind for you?

Where does the 3M 'awesome purpose' fit in the hierarchy? It is a major objective.

Exercise: What is the most inspiring vision you have ever heard of in any organisation? When have you been most switched on at work? What was the awesome purpose behind your motivation? Was it your own personal one, or an organisation-wide awesome purpose?

GETTING IT WRONG

Here is a particularly bad vision statement: 'the one others copy'. It is one of Mobil's. Where is the tangible end point? Where is the thing that employees can see? Where is the human advance? It fails, and failed to work. Why? Because like thousands of others of a similar ilk, it is a platitude. It says what everybody says: 'We want to be the best.' Who does not? To be the best, you must achieve something that makes you the best. Where is that something in this vision statement? Without a clear point focused on one outcome, you do not have an awesome purpose, you have a platitude.

Exercise: Here is a better (but not perfect) awesome purpose from AT&T: 'to be our customer's best sales relationship'. Why is it better? What is still wrong with it? At which position in the CAM would this fit best?

Back to the New York railways. All has not gone well. The momentum has been lost. The organisation is now focusing on trying to reduce delays, a laudable goal. Specifically, the tactic they have adopted is to attack the mean time between failures. But at the time of writing, this programme has not been as successful as 'No Graffiti.' Why? It breaks the rules. There is no awesome purpose. People don't leap out of bed electrified by the thought of reducing the mean time between failures by 1 per cent. So what would work for them? Well, whatever it is, it must apply to their interest groups, it must be inspiring, it must be memorable, it must take into account the existing culture and the company's recent history. What do customers want? They want to get to their destination on time. Addressing mean time between failures looks at only one cause of delays; there are many at every stage in the customer handling process. What would work as an awesome purpose? 'No Delays.'

AWESOME PURPOSES AND EXPERIMENTATION

OK, so now you have this great vision, this spine-tingling awesome purpose. You can see where you want to go, but since nobody has been there before, there is no road map. In day-to-day life, what do you do if you want to get from A to B without a road map. You ask whoever you think might be able to throw some light on the situation from their local knowledge. Finding your route to achieve the vision is exactly the same. You ask those who might have a little bit of the whole map you are trying to create.

What if there is no one to ask? What then? You would set off in the general direction and take whatever twists and turns you thought may be closest to your desired direction. Eventually, you get there. How? By trial and error. By a combination of forethought and experimentation.

ASSUMPTION CHECKS

Visions are supported and built on certain assumptions. When you are seeking to establish a vision, you would be wise to also articulate those assumptions. Then document them. When you periodically review your progress toward the vision, also review the assumptions on which it is based. Check them against the current commercial realities. You will quickly see how rapidly assumptions become outdated. On what assumptions is your current mission or vision based?

SELL-BEFORE DATE

Vision, missions and awesome purposes only work to the point where they have been achieved or are about to be achieved. Then they must be replaced by a new awesome purpose to keep the organisation aligned, focused and stimulated. As your awesome purpose reaches completion, you must be looking for another. People hate being without purpose; they become listless and depressed. To quote a rather famous text on successful living: 'Without purpose, the people will perish.' As a leader or future leader of people, it is your responsibility to make sure they have what they need in order to perform.

THE LEADER OF VISIONS

A hallmark of a good leader is the ability to steer the course between the ideal of the vision and the daily realities of business without undermining the importance of the vision. How is it done? All decisions must be made with reference to the vision, *and* be seen to be so made. Many short-term expediencies will present themselves. Tempting opportunities to ignore the vision for some quick advantage will come thick and fast. If you choose, take those that help towards the vision, and ignore those that do not: you will send a strong signal to all concerned that pursuing the vision is the priority. Your staff will copy you. But if you start indulging yourself in these little temptations, it won't be long before all your staff follow your lead and your culture is as poorly focused as it was before you set the vision.

Whoever leads the vision or mission must have as much to lose as those who are led, preferably more. S/he who leads the vision must epitomise it. For example, if you are leading a campaign to remove corruption from public life, you must be squeaky clean. You must either have no skeletons in your closet or already have taken them all out for public inspection and left the door open for anyone who wishes to inspect, any time they wish.

SUMMARY

For team alignment to truly take place, each individual member of the team must be in tune with the collective vision. Indeed, there is no collective vision if each member is not voluntarily in tune with one agreed end point. Such alignment can only exist if all the key players have been involved in the process of arriving at the vision, or if the vision is so in tune with the shared values that there is no doubt that everyone will buy into it. Then it must be expressed in some way that captures people's imagination. It should ideally send shivers down spines.

8 Strategy

CHAPTER OVERVIEW

- The status quo
- Strategy demystified
- Getting to be number one
- The Four-layer Strategy Model
- The growth myth
- Strategy and the CAM
- Strategy and experimentation
- The status quo continued
- Formulating a strategy in the absence of an awesome purpose
- The benefit dimensions approach to strategy
- Strategy-formation with the CAM
- Choosing and checking, working and maintaining
- Persistence: Making your strategy work
- The Strategy Monitoring and Improvement group
- Getting it wrong, getting it right
- Chapter summary
- Part summary

The objectives of this chapter are to demystify strategy, to explain how it derives from the higher levels of the CAM, and to explain how to arrive at a strategy in the absence of the CAM.

THE STATUS QUO

The vast majority of organisations have no strategy. They are opportunistic. Consequently, they find it difficult to target potential customers – they don't know who or where their customers are.

Even in those companies that do have a strategy, it is rarely known amongst the staff. Going up a performance division to those companies that do have a disseminated strategy, it is rarely clear and even more rarely in line with the organisation's vision, if it has one.

Exercise: Without looking it up, state your organisation's strategy in one sentence – in one *short* sentence.

STRATEGY-FORMATION IS REQUIRED WHEN . . .

This point will be controversial. If you do not want your blood pressure raised, skip the rest of this paragraph. The more I work in this field, the clearer it becomes that only those companies which do not have a clear vision need to spend a lot of time on strategy. Those companies which have an awesome purpose, those companies which have some 'advance the human race' type vision never have any problems with strategy. Since Intel adopted their purpose to continually advance computer processing power, their strategy has been simple and devastatingly effective: to continually produce faster and more processing power at the same or lower prices. The competition no sooner climb the mountain and catch up than they find themselves at the bottom starting all over again. Intel have undisputed leadership in the industry by seeking to provide the most processing power at the lowest price humanity has ever seen.

Exercise: If your company has no awesome purpose, list the process that was last used to generate your strategy.

BEYOND SEEKING TO TWEAK: THE DIMINISHING RETURNS OF INCREMENTALISM

Most companies which have a strategy eventually slip into incrementalism: instead of looking for new, more effective ways to deliver an awesome benefit, they seek to tweak the existing strategy. Of course, you should be trying to improve your strategy on an ongoing basis, but not to the point where you never examine the basis for the strategy you are trying to improve.

Incremental improvements to what is offered are no longer enough to take a huge market share. Yes, you can continue to improve your products and processes, but the law of diminishing returns applies to that approach. Only when you do something radically different do you set yourself apart from the also-rans. If you are not leading, you are following. The best you can ever be as a follower is number two. If you are in business in order to be number two or if you are in business just to make a living, do me a favour: put this book down now. It is not written for you. But if you are in business to win, welcome to the starting blocks.

Exercise: If your company has an articulated strategy, how long has it been in force?

HIGHEST-LEVEL STRATEGIC THINKERS

The highest-level strategic thinkers either create new industries or completely re-invent existing ones. They are mavericks; they break the rules. Well, that is how it appears to their competitors, but not to their customers. They are, in fact, playing the game according to the rules their customers have, but which previously were not articulated.

These so-called mavericks are industry-makers because usually they buy into George Bernard Shaw's observation:

> You see things; and you say, 'Why?' But I see things that never were; and I say 'Why not?'

Of course, these people are not really engaging in any high, rocket science-level strategic thinking. Their strategy is blindingly obvious from the awesome purpose they have set.

Commercial success is about providing that which is not provided, or providing it in a way in which it is not provided. Successful strategies go where the compliant herd-followers fear to tread. Ironically, those companies which are best equipped with the resources to take the lead with ground-breaking strategies are those least equipped to adopt them, because of their inertia and moribund cultures. Most ground-breaking strategies come from new players in most fields. The future is created by them, and is therefore for them. The future is rarely created by the old guard. The old guard forefeit their claim on the future as soon as they start following, rather than making, the rules of the market.

In the race to build the future, are you crinkly or crisp, frazzled or fresh? Do you epitomise inertia or initiative? Are you the stunning architecture of the new, or the rubble of the old? Are you Wellington or Napoleon, Churchill or Hitler? Are you the hedgehog or the truck? The eagle or its prey? Man or mouse?

Exercise: Consider your industry. Bring to mind the top five most effective business offerings in the last few years. How many of them were initiatives by the old guard?

STRATEGY DEMYSTIFIED

Strategy is incredibly simple. Yet book after book is published on the subject. Instead of casting light on it, they bury it in jargon and confuse everyone involved.

Strategy is simple. You either:

- attack
- consolidate
- retreat

Having decided on one of those three, you then have another simple choice:

attack through products, operations or total solutions? Then you have another simple choice: attack by being better, cheaper or faster? Better, cheaper or faster can be interpreted to suit specific markets, but that is the basic choice. Now, can you put your hand on your heart and tell me you need a complex model to see your way through that?

If you can't, then create the model you think is required. Then compare it to the simple but effective model on page 114.

HOW AND WHERE DO YOU ATTACK?

The great war strategist Von Clausewitz advises that a successful attacking strategy:

- employs all your available forces with the maximum energy
- concentrates your force at the place where you are most likely to win
- is rapid; it wastes no time – speed of execution of a strategy is more important than the tactics within the strategy

Focusing your resources on one point

In business language, that means using your unique competence to provide a benefit that a viable number of customers want in a specified market about which you have superior knowledge. 'Unique competence' may appear to be a bit of a misnomer. There may be others with the same competencies, but as long as they are operating in different markets or in different locations, you can think of yours as unique competencies.

Unique competencies are not the same as values. Marks & Spencer have excellent supplier-management competencies, but supplier management is not a central value, neither is it a purpose, vision or mission. In the CAM, their supplier-management competencies would cover the span from a major objective, tactic, objectives and operating principles.

Strategy applies your unique competencies in the most powerful and market-aligned way the mission can be achieved. Tactics are the way in which you achieve Von Clausewitz's criteria. You will have a range of tactics to employ all your available forces with the maximum energy. You will have tactics to concentrate your force in the way specified by the strategy (better, faster, cheaper). You will have tactics to move quickly.

Unassailable positions?

The ultimate strategic victory is to have your competitors concede without a fight because they believe that your position is so strong. But as any decent entrepreneur will tell you, there is no such thing as an unassailable position. Small-time entrepreneurs have taken on corporate giants and beaten them into the ground on innumerable occasions. The thing that usually undoes large organisations is their lack of responsiveness. Big organisations just cannot move fast enough to respond to changes in the marketplace. The entrepreneur usually has a greenfield site. S/he does not have to spend huge amounts of time and money changing an old and outdated structure. S/he is not faced with the dilemma of scrapping expensive machinery or systems before they have paid for themselves because there is now a better way of doing things. The entrepreneur can adopt the most effective systems and machinery for today's commercial environment unencumbered by the baggage of yesterday. It is often faster and less costly to set up an organisation from scratch to deliver something than to try to change an existing one.

Exercise: Name three situations in which you know an entrepreneur has knocked the top players off their slots.

IMMOBILITY

If entrepreneurs are regularly able to beat the big players because of the latter group's unresponsiveness, it might be smart to examine·where and how your competitors are unresponsive.

Spot what your competitors won't change. Spot the point at which your competitors are rigid, either by design or default. In martial arts, as soon as an opponent has lifted a foot off the ground to make a kicking attack, they are committed to the foot still on the ground. They are rigid by necessity at that point of contact with the ground. Most counter-attacks use the point of rigidity to their advantage (there are, of course, exceptions to that). Where are your competitors immobile? What are they committed to keeping constant? How can you turn that to your advantage? Are they so committed to quality that they can never deliver speed? Are they so committed to speed they can never deliver customer compassion? Are they so committed to compassion that they can never deliver cheaply? Are they so committed to low prices that they can never invest in improved products? Are they . . .? Got the idea?

Exercise: What are your competitors tied to, thereby rendering them vulnerable? What are you tied to?

STRENGTH AGAINST WEAKNESS

Successful strategies are always a concentration of strength against weakness or total absence of strategy. Great strategies always avoid taking on your competitor's strengths. Head-to-heads are rarely worthwhile for either party. The only people who benefit from head-to-heads are the customers (who pick up the short-lived bargains as both parties reduce prices or increase what is offered for the same price) and your mutual competitors. They will be rubbing their hands with glee. For, as the two Goliaths grind each other down, the David is planning, waiting for the moment to strike, the moment when the two Goliaths are too weak to defend themselves.

The David may not have even been born when the Goliaths start on each other. The David company may be created specifically to take advantage of the changed balance of power.

You can pit strength against weakness in several ways. But in the final analysis, each strategy boils down to better, faster or cheaper for any specified market group.

If the competitor is slow, you could go for speed. If they go for cheap and cheerful, you could go for speed. If they provide nationwide coverage, you could go for the largest regional areas only (not having the overheads associated with having to cover low-profit areas). If they cater for the mass market, you could go for the speciality market. If they go for economies of scale, you could go for the personalised service approach. If they go for . . .

Exercise: What strategies do each of your competitors use? Where does that leave them exposed?

The same product can be sold using different strategies.

In my work, I regularly come across two incorrect assumptions. First, that a company's strategy has to be unique. It does not. It cannot be. With only three options to choose from, how could it be? The benefit you are seeking to deliver is ideally unique, but the strategy need not be. Second, that the same product must be sold using the same strategies. That is not so. For instance, there are two major credit card companies offering ostensibly identical products doing so using different strategies. AMEX sells elitism and privilege. Visa sells ubiquity. Both claim to be better in some specified way.

Exercise: List ten companies in your industry. Does each have a unique strategy, or can they be categorised into better, faster, cheaper? List ten companies that sell apparently identical products or services. Note the variation in their strategies.

WHO DEFINES A SUCCESSFUL STRATEGY?

Many companies behave as though they believe that they can make themselves successful. They cannot. The only people who can make your company successful are your clients. The only way they are going to do that is if you provide them with something no one else can provide, if your unique competence is sufficiently distinctive to make it smart for the customer to come to you to get what s/he wants.

GETTING TO BE NUMBER ONE

Leadership in any marketplace occurs when the customer's expectations are substantially exceeded. When what is provided at the price it is provided at cannot be readily explained by the customer. Leadership occurs when the customer is in awe of what you can do for them. Leadership occurs when you come close to fulfilling your awesome purpose. Leadership is granted by customers when you deliver an awesome benefit.

Leadership occurs when your competitors are competing on today's playing field while you have already mastered the rules of tomorrow. Leadership occurs when your competitors have expertise in their industry, expertise which is, *de facto*, expertise in yesterday's best practices, and you are creating the expertise of tomorrow's best practices. Leadership occurs when others are reaching benchmarks while you are creating them.

If you want to be number one, you must lead. If you want to lead, you must go into unknown territory. If you go into unknown territory, you will experiment and make mistakes. Those experiments and mistakes will give you the knowledge that put you ahead. There is no choice in the matter. Supreme success means making supreme mistakes, and supreme mistakes give you the information you need for supreme success.

If you are to be number one in your field, you have to provide your category of provision better than anyone else. It is as simple as that. You are either number one or you are an also-ran. And if you are not shooting to be number one, if you are not shooting to do something better, faster, cheaper than ever before, you *are* shooting to be an also-ran.

You do not have to be a product development company to be number one; many people assume that you have to be. McDonald's has dominated the world of convenience food for a very long time. Why? They produce that type of food more efficiently (better) than anyone else on earth. They have the best food quality assurance methods in their industry. Well, perhaps until recently. Rally's in the USA is even more efficient. How? Burt Sugarman, the founder, realised that despite the public perception that the big hamburger companies were in the fast food business, they were not that fast. So Rally's worked on speed (faster) as their strategy. How did that pan out at the operational level? They provide only 11 menu items, no seating – drive-through or walk-up service only, and a maximum delivery time of 45 seconds or you get it free. Now that's speed, that's efficiency. How successful have they been? Many hundreds of outlets over the USA and a turnover of many hundreds of millions of dollars, and still growing! I do not know what their awesome purpose was, but if it was to provide the fastest high-quality fast food in human history, they certainly have achieved it. I hope they have set another one.

What if you are a company aiming neither at being operationally better nor faster nor aiming at providing a better product. What if you are aiming at providing a better overall service, the best overall service ever? What if you are

111

positioning yourself for total solution superiority? IBM did, and were extremely successful for many decades, until they became bureaucratically overloaded. The best overall service as a strategy is not limited to IBM. By seeking to provide the best total IT solutions from systems analysis to computer risk assurance, that strategy has taken CSF (Computer Services and Finance plc in the UK) from 0 to £45 million turnover in just seven years.

The point is, it does not matter whether your strategic value proposition (your specific interpretation of better, faster, cheaper) is product superiority, operational superiority or total solutions superiority. What matters is that you know what your strategy is, and that it is driven by your vision to provide the 'best ever' in some way, in your market.

Exercise: Are you seeking to be faster, cheaper or better in product, operational or total service terms?

CATEGORIES OF BENEFIT

Any strategy (better, faster, cheaper) can be further broken down into categories of benefit. For instance, you may be providing the best washing powder product, then someone starts providing the best clothes-protection washing powder. Someone else starts providing the best environmentally friendly washing powder. Then someone else starts providing the best clothes-protecting, environmentally friendly washing powder.

Can you see how the market has been gradually segmented into benefit categories? Can you see how even though all the products are following the 'best strategy', each is trying to be best in a particular category? Can you also see that each product is providing its own awesome benefit? And that, as a result, each is creating its own market.

If you have an awesome purpose, you will automatically know what awesome benefit you are providing, and that, in turn, will dictate your strategy. (For an example, take a look at our hypothetical instruments company on pages 60–61.)

THE FOUR-LAYER STRATEGY MODEL

A STRATEGY MODEL, OR COMMON SENSE?

So far, we have discussed a range of choices that you have as you consider what strategy you will adopt in order to pursue your awesome purpose. Normally it is the other way around: the awesome purpose will choose the strategy. But it is useful to understand the range of choices in relation to each other, for if you cannot come up with an awesome purpose, you still have a business to run. You still need a means by which to choose a strategy. So let's recap on the analysis behind the model before laying out the synthesis which is the Four-layer Strategy Model.

As I said, strategy is simple: you either attack, consolidate or retreat. Since you can only ever acquire leadership by attacking, and since this is not a book on strategy, we will ignore the other two.

We have also noted that there are three ways to convey a benefit: via product superiority, operational superiority, or total solution superiority.

Strategy, then, is broken down in to one of three benefit options: better, faster or cheaper.

Finally, the benefit options can be broken down into benefit categories (see the diagram of the Four-layer Strategy Model on page 114).

Companies with an awesome purpose seeking to provide an awesome benefit find their position in the model established for them by their previous thinking: the thinking which led them to their awesome purpose.

Of course, this model is also used to analyse the market as it currently stands. Look at all the players in the marketplace, categorise them into 'Product', 'Operational' or 'Total Solution' providers. Then further categorise them into those competing on the basis of better, faster and cheaper. Finally, list each of these under the benefit category they provide.

Having completed the market analysis, you can then start thinking about what is and is not provided. You may find that there is no 'Total Solutions' provider in the market, or perhaps that everyone is competing on the basis of product superiority and that no one is providing acceptable products in an operationally superior way, or that everyone is going for operational superiority but no one has a superior product.

You may find that in the benefit categories provided, no one has addressed the 'ease of use' category. Perhaps there is a huge disabled persons' market out there which would use a variant of the product. That product would then form a new category – the best product for disabled users (that benefit category can further be broken down into products for the range of disability types). Or perhaps you will find that no one has addressed the 'easiest to assemble' benefit category. Or perhaps the 'most portable' benefit category crown remains unclaimed. Or perhaps the 'fastest maintenance' trophy is gathering dust in some judge's room.

Can you see how useful a tool this could be for you? Perhaps I am too heavy on the conditions under which strategy analysis is required. Maybe you could use the Four-layer Strategy Model to help you find your awesome purpose. Yes, if you must. But bear this in mind: you may find a wonderful niche in the market by taking this approach, but will it match your values? If you choose one that does not match your values, and those of your staff, you are making a bed of nails for yourself. Not only will you have to do things which you just don't believe in, but you will have to watch your competitors doing those things better because they *do* believe in them. How awesome is your deliverable benefit going to be if you don't have your heart in it?

It is much better to search for your awesome purpose the other way round: identify your values, distil your purpose, visualise a future and so on, as

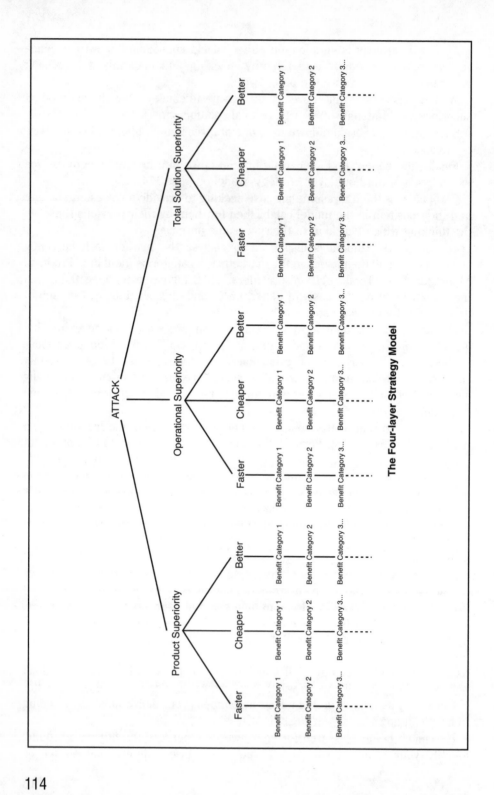

The Four-layer Strategy Model

114

previously described, and then position yourself in the Four-layer Strategy Model for the purposes of market-monitoring.

Exercise: How will you use the Four-layer Strategy Model to monitor your marketplace?

THE GROWTH MYTH

What are the much discussed 'high-growth strategies'? High growth comes from matching your unique competence with emerging trends and high-growth sectors of the economy. What causes emerging trends? Someone somewhere has found a way of providing a benefit much faster, cheaper or better than anyone else, to the extent that people who would not previously have purchased whatever it is now find it worth buying.

Growth comes from delivering an awesome benefit. Many companies seek growth in a ritualistic way. They crucify themselves on the cross of growth without ever realising that it is customers who create growth, and awesome benefit creates customers. Like you, I have explored countless 'strategic tools', most of which offer some quantitative way of coming up (supposedly) with the perfect strategy. One has been presented here. Some are useful, but most are little more than intellectual masturbation aids. The most important element of a successful strategy is finding an awesome purpose and delivering an awesome benefit.

If you can't come up with an awesome benefit (keep trying), you will have to content yourself with second best until you do. Achieve second place by focusing on what your organisation does best and do it better, or do only what you do best, or more of what you do best. Achieve second place by seeking incremental improvements, and by following the existing rules.

If you are having difficulty finding an awesome purpose or awesome benefit, do not slip into self-doubt and start assuming that one does not exist. It does. It is just that your current perception of the market does not allow you to see it (or, more likely, see *them*). If you do reach that point of dispair, you should refer to the reframing section (see pages 180–192), or get in touch with me.

Perhaps the ideal target markets to which to apply your resources, with the greatest likelihood of success, are the high-growth sectors of the economy. The fastest-growing companies have clients in fast-growing sectors of the economy and/or other fast-growing companies as their clients. It easier to go up in a rising tide.

What do you do if you are not in a growth market and have not been able to come up with an awesome benefit to make your market grow? What do you do if you are in a mature market?

Two classic strategic options in an established or mature market are: cost advantage (cheaper) and differentiation ('better' in some specific perceived way appropriate to a particular sector of the market – not usually 'better' in real terms).

What makes a mature market? Could it be that no one has innovated in the market for some time? Could it be that there are many players all offering pretty much the same thing? Could it be that there is a serious case of herd mentality throughout the industry? Could it be that you are in a market just waiting to be shaken up; just waiting for someone to offer some wonderful new benefit – an awesome benefit?

Exercise: If you are in a mature market, what is your current strategy? What wonderful new benefit would capture a bigger share of that sleeping giant?

STRATEGY AND THE CAM

Successful companies are bonded to their successful culture, not to any product, not to any service, not to any strategy, not to any vision. Although all of these things are important, the company is willing to change them, but not the culture. Strategy and all the lower levels of the CAM must always be subservient to culture (values and purpose). We will come back to this point in more detail later.

In addition, workable strategies should be constantly evolving and rapidly turning into major objectives, tactics and objectives by those who will be executing the strategy. Great strategies must be phrased in a way which lets everyone in the company know where to compete, and also tells them how you define the company's superiority.

Strategies work when they are aligned with the market, when they are aligned with the organisational values, when they are aligned with the vision and mission, and when they draw on the unique competencies of the organisation (or to a lesser extent, when they establish appropriate competencies).

STRATEGY AND EXPERIMENTATION

To arrive (temporarily) at a successful strategy, you must be prepared to experiment. If you are experimenting, you must be prepared for failures. If you are failing, you must be prepared to learn from those failures. If you are learning from your failures, you must be prepared to succeed. If you are going through the cycle just drawn, on a regular basis, you must be prepared to succeed big time.

THE STATUS QUO CONTINUED

STRATEGY-FORMATION

Most companies have a grossly inadequate way of reviewing and formulating strategy. The board meeting does not lend itself to providing enough time. Strategy, if it gets a mention at all in the customary full agenda, will get a brief slot. Also problematic is the process of raising strategy in board meetings. The chairperson usually forms the agenda, and normally takes the view, rightfully, that implementing the strategy successfully is of greater importance than picking at its flaws. All very well, assuming the flaws are not fatal. Taking issue with the strategy is usually taken personally by the leaders of a company. It is seen as a frontal assault on their competence.

So how can strategy be effectively examined, reviewed or even changed? Usually only when the wolf is at the door with its last victim's blood still on its teeth is the company forced to look at change.

The wolf may come in many forms: a takeover threat, a threatening new competitor (see the realisation section, pages 167–173, for more details of what forces change) or many others.

If you are not pursuing an awesome purpose, trying to deliver awesome benefits, you don't have a strategy; you have tactics. You are not a strategist, you are a tactician. Tacticians may win some battles, but never the war. Now, if you are a strategist *and* a tactician, that is quite a different matter.

Conventional strategy planning looks at yesterday in order to plan tomorrow. A sound, prudent accounting approach to that ensures you are in the game, but not winning the game; following the rules, but not making them. Those who play not to lose rarely win.

Market dominance is only ever achieved and maintained by delivering more tomorrow than customers get today. Tomorrow is never created by processing the figures of yesterday. Strictly, that is not true; if your tomorrow is created by analysis of yesterday, the tomorrow you create will always play second fiddle to those with awesome purpose, to those who create the future.

PLANNING NEVER CREATES STRATEGY

Most current strategy planning is about how to operate successfully within the limits of what is. Only when you move towards thinking of what could be, only when you move towards envisioning what might be, will you move from being a left-overs taker to a future-maker. Planning never produces a winning strategy. Only visioning, creating an awesome purpose can do that. Once you have your strategy, planning finds its place – to document the allocation and use of resources in order to achieve the awesome purpose by using the method spelled out in the strategy, with the values guiding the overall process.

FORMULATING A STRATEGY IN THE ABSENCE OF AN AWESOME PURPOSE

Successful strategy, like awesome purpose, is not arrived at by a few boffins locked away in a cupboard somewhere until it's time to bring them out. Usually, strategy emerges from experimentation. That is not to imply that analysis is useless. Quite the contrary. Analysis is the stage which designs the experiments, and the stage after experimentation in which the results are interpreted. None the less, the strategy will emerge in the light of market reactions, not solely from protracted spreadsheet calculations.

Successful strategies emerge from a variety of ideas. If you have created an organisation full of clones with no diversity and no new ideas coming in, you have created an organisation like 16-year-olds who leave school thinking that their education is finished; no new ideas are required to make progress. Or perhaps like the village population which refuses to allow marriage outside its own confines. You end up with a 50-year-old idiot with a 16-year-old's brain and a village full of inbred morons, respectively.

UNDERSTANDING THE PROCESS

How can you learn about strategic thinking process? By choosing a commercial environment about which you, safely, know nothing. One in which you are not burdened by your knowledge of the industry; what is possible and what is not. Losing that burden will free your mind to examine the process of strategic thinking.

- Choose an industry other than your own.
- Choose a sector within that industry.
- Choose a deliverable, a product or service.
- Identify which benefits the customers are buying and how they like to buy them.
- Break down those observations into market segments.

Then start asking questions:

- What benefit, in that sector, would customers consider attractive if you could deliver it?
- What is the gap between what is possible now and that benefit?
- How could you provide something that is part way to crossing that gap?

That is your strategy.

Try this simple loop on several different industries until you are comfortable that you understand and can use the thinking process without prompting:

- In which markets are you seeking to compete?
- What industry are you in?
- What sector are you operating in?
- What are your deliverables?
- What information do you need to assess that marketplace?
- What benefits are the customers buying, and how do they like to buy them?
- How is the market segmented? What is provided in what way to create each segment?
- Who are the players in each segment, particularly in the one you currently operate within?
- What do they deliver and how? What are their strategies?
- What value is it that the customer obtains or thinks s/he obtains from buying the competitor's offering? What drives buying behaviour in each segment of the marketplace?
- Where is the largest segment of the market?
- The delivery of what in what way would be superior in each segment?
- How could your unique competence be used to deliver those things?
- What would you have to add to your unique competencies to deliver that thing?
- In which segment are you in the best position to take leadership?
- Going back up to the sector level, what benefit in that sector would all customers consider attractive if you could deliver it?

- What is the gap between what is possible now and that benefit?
- How could you provide something that is part way to crossing that gap?

That is your strategy.

Exercise: The above has obviously been written to cover all sorts of companies in all sorts of situations. Change it, tailor it to suit your company in your situation.

THE BENEFIT DIMENSION APPROACH TO STRATEGY

Previously we looked at the Four-layer Strategy Model and noted that each strategy can be broken down into benefit categories. The dimensional approach to strategy is a tool for identifying which benefits customers most value. The conclusions of this analysis may even lead you to identify a whole new benefit category. Let's see how.

VALUE DIMENSION

Ask questions about what benefit dimensions or elements of the products/ services customers care about. Ask questions about how much customers value each benefit dimension (BD). Ask questions about how much customers perceive they are paying for each BD. Ask questions about how much each BD costs to produce. Ask questions about what proportion of customers seeks each BD; how each BD is used as a buying criterion in each major segment of the market. Which of your competitors provides the best value in each of these BDs? What would customers consider to be superior value to the best currently provided on each of those BDs?

The benefit dimension analysis table below gives a format to help you with the first stage of the BD analysis approach.

The benefit analysis dimension table

Purchase Price	Value Dimension	% of Value Attributed by Customer	Volume of Dimension to Customer	A Value of Dimension to Customer	B Cost of Provision to Us	% of Total Cost per Dimension	Cost: Value (B/A) per Dimension
£Y	D1	75	Y*0.75	£	R	%	R/£
	D2	15	Y*0.15	£	S	%	S/£
	D3 ...	5	Y*0.05	£	T	%	T/£

Each leading company owns in the mind of the customer the perception of being the best provider of a benefit category: a group of specific benefit dimensions. IBM, until recently, owned the benefit category 'best total solutions in computing'. Rolls-Royce own the benefit category 'highest-status hand-made luxury cars'. McDonald's own the benefit 'high-quality convenience food'. Intel own the dimension group/benefit category 'best-value computer chips'. The dimension group you seek to own in the minds of the customer will be obvious from your awesome purpose. If it is not, you can use this method to identify the dimensions of the benefits which customers most want.

COST DIMENSION

Making any purchase has a cost above and beyond the financial exchange between buyer and seller. The total cost includes: less than perfect reliability; service costs; mistakes, delays; purchase time; other purchasing activity cost, and the actual financial transaction. Customers consider the cost dimensions as well as the benefit dimensions they seek. If you know what the cost dimensions are, you can seek to provide customers with superior value by reducing or eliminating them. The success of the Dyson vacuum cleaner is based at least partly on the elimination of some costs, and therefore the reduction in total costs of purchase and ownership.

Use the same format to that above to calculate how much negative value customers place on each buying cost or inconvenience. What could you provide that removes the perception of cost from the customer, and thus makes doing business with you more beneficial than anyone else, or at a lower total cost than anyone else?

An ideal point of attack is one where the customer's costs of doing business are high or perceived to be high and you remove them for what, to you, is a small cost. Having explored which customer costs you can reduce most cost-effectively, you can then combine that information with your decision on which benefit dimensions to focus on to give you a lead.

Exercise: What products have you bought recently? Conduct as much of the dimensional analysis on yourself as possible (obviously, you won't have access to the costing information).

PROBLEMS WITH PAST-FACING STRATEGY-FORMATION TECHNIQUES

Bear in mind that if a market can be researched, it is an old market. If you are looking at information that can be gained about an old market, you probably don't have an awesome purpose. If you have to generate your own information, you are likely to be cutting new ground. That is assuming that you have not overlooked some available data. Another caution for you: be very wary of researching markets on the basis of seeking the ingredients of the ideal products or service. Ford did exactly that with the infamous Edsel. They spent hundreds of millions of dollars trying to come up with the ideal mid-range car, produced it and found no one wanted it because it was so symbolic of Mr and Mrs Average.

While the mid-range of any market *is* where the largest group of customers are, none of them like to feel that they are like sheep in a giant pen. They all want to feel catered for as individuals (even if they are all treated exactly the same).

As stated previously, this kind of analysis is only conducted when there is an absence of some 'humanity improvement' vision, some awesome purpose. But that is not to say that it cannot be used to come up with such a vision. It can. By knowing where the customer perceives the greatest value to lie, by knowing where customers feel the true costs of doing business lie, you can generate a highly successful vision or awesome purpose.

Amstrad, the UK-based computer company, was so successful because it provided the central core of what customers wanted without the frills and other unwanted costs other computer companies were providing. They provided, amongst other things, a highly successful range of word-processing computers. If you wanted only a word processor, Amstrad could provide one at less than a fifth of the cost that other computer companies would charge you for a word processor and a thousand and one other things that were of no use and of no interest to you.

STRATEGY-FORMATION WITH THE CAM

The best way to devise a strategy is to arrive at an awesome purpose, in the way laid out in Chapter 7. If you have set an awesome purpose, your choice of strategy will be fairly straightforward. 3M's stated purpose is to solve unsolved problems. We have aleady discussed that they have chosen to pursue that purpose in the direction of technology. From even those two stages in the CAM, their strategy is already set and entirely obvious: to find unsolved problems and develop technical solutions to them. Their strategy is to develop products to solve problems (better).

Taking our idealised instruments company. Their strategy was set the moment the vision and values were established. So their strategy had to be: 'provide the easiest to install and most maintenance-free instruments (cheaper – lower overall cost)'.

Exercise: Look at the major advances in your industry. What was the strategy behind them?

The best way to arrive at a strategy is to let it 'drop out' of the awesome purpose-formation process. Yes, I know it sounds like an uncontrolled process, but as you can see above, it works. The process is as follows:

- What are our values?
- What is our purpose?
- In which direction are we pursuing our purpose?
- What is our vision?
- What is our mission?
- What is our awesome purpose?
- What awesome benefit does that suggest we are going to deliver to our customers, and how?

That is your strategy.

If you are used to the endless analysis that goes on in most big companies, it will sound trite or even ridiculous suggesting that strategy will just 'drop out' of a process, but it does. If you find a strong enough 'why' and a clear enough 'what', the 'how' is usually blindingly obvious. Answer the following questions to see what I mean.

If you wanted to get to the South Pole, how would you do it? If you wanted to put a cherry on top of the Eiffel Tower, how would you do it? If you wanted to put a man on the moon, how would you do it? If you wanted to have a Coke™ within arm's reach of everyone on the planet, how would you do it? If you wanted to encircle Caterpillar, how would you do it?

How (strategy) is always obvious when the 'why' and 'what' are strongly in place. The 'formation' of great strategies is more about the formation of awesome purpose than about any fancy analysis.

CHOOSING AND CHECKING, WORKING AND MAINTAINING

CHOOSING AND CHECKING

If you have sought to formulate your strategy using conventional techniques, you may have generated a few strategy options, several points of attack on the marketplace. Which do you go for? How do you decide what strategy to choose? The best answer is to ask a few questions which break down the larger question into manageable chunks. This quick checklist also doubles as a means of checking that your strategy is sound.

Internal checks

- How does the strategy match your company purpose?
- How does the strategy match your organisational values (actual, not espoused)?
- How does the strategy match the direction in which you have chosen to pursue your purpose?
- How does the strategy match your company vision?
- How does the strategy match your organisation's mission?
- How does the strategy match and draw on your unique competencies?

- How does the strategy match your awesome purpose?
- Does the proposed strategy give you a clear 'how to offer something' that no one else is offering?
- Does the proposed strategy seek to deliver an awesome benefit? Does it seek to do so faster, cheaper, better . . .?
- Is the strategy clear and simple?
- Have you been able to turn it into simple, achievable major objectives?
- Can you put more or better resources or methods into the focal point of the strategy?
- What resources will be required to execute this strategy?
- Do you have them, or can you acquire them (resources: appropriate culture; people; skills; finance; materials; equipment, etc.)
- Will it provide efficiencies in the use of resources?

External checks

- Does the strategy offer you some protection from your competitors' realistic counter-moves?
- Does the strategy attack an area you know your competitors won't move into, either because it would take them away from their core business or it would force them to contradict themselves in the eyes of the customers?
- Can the strategy be implemented quickly, and will it come as a surprise to the opposition?
- How does the strategy tune into high-growth areas?
- Does it give you leadership of a key product or service benefit category?
- Can the way of delivering your product or service (strategy) be managed as a potential brand?
- Does it have the potential to attract publicity?
- Will it give existing customers a feel-good buzz?
- Does it offer the potential to tie customers to you?
- Does it offer the potential for customers to seek other products or services from you?

Does your proposed strategy match all of the above? If so, it may be the best strategy for you. If you are in the lucky position of having several workable strategies coming through the above checks, what do you do? Choose the one that best matches your values and purpose. And if several can be deemed to match equally well, if all will provide an awesome benefit that will give you a commanding lead, what do you do? You must go for the one that your culture is best equipped to deliver – as your culture is now. How do you make that decision? Go further down the CAM hierarchy asking questions about whether the strategy matches what you currently have in place.

PERSISTENCE: MAKING YOUR STRATEGY WORK

Whatever strategy pops out of whatever process, you must commit yourself to sticking to its general thrust; unless of course it is proving to be unsuccessful. But success with any strategy takes time. Many companies go to extraordinary lengths to formulate a strategy, and put only a fraction of that effort into implementing it. Result: a good strategy falls on its face. Making strategies work is much, much tougher than coming up with them in the first place. Part of that success comes from getting the entire organisation using the same 'how to'. Until the organisation is pointing in the same direction using the same 'how to', it is difficult to say whether the strategy is working properly or the organisation is properly working the strategy.

Here are a few very obvious tips on making a strategy work:

- Put in place everything that is needed to make your hard-found strategy work.
- Put all the available resources behind making the strategy work (this tip should come as no surprise given that we have defined strategy as the means by which the organisation directs its resources to achieve its vision).
- The people who will implement the strategy are those who should plan its implementation.
- A brilliant implementation of an OK plan beats an OK implementation of a brilliant plan hands down.
- Make rewards for behaviour fit the values, awesome purpose and be in line with the strategy.
- Give people responsibility within the guidelines the awesome purpose, values and strategy lay down.

Exercise: What measures will you put in place to determine when and to what extent the culture is aligned behind the strategy?

EXPOSING UNDERLYING ASSUMPTIONS

What are the underlying assumptions in your industry? If you don't know what they are, how can you challenge them? How can you break the rules if they unconsciously control all your actions? By uncovering the assumptions and articulating them, you will be in a position to examine their current validity. They were probably made many years ago, and have probably gone unexamined since they were widely adopted. If you can identify those which are outdated in the minds of customers but widely held in the minds of the industry, you can move towards providing an awesome benefit.

STICK TO YOUR VISION/MISSION/AWESOME PURPOSE

Listen to old Pareto: 80 per cent of what will make any strategy work will be the core 20 per cent. Identify the 20 per cent that will get most of your results. But don't forget the other stuff; you don't want to find yourself in a 'for the sake of a nail we lost the shoe, for the sake of the shoe we lost the horse, for the sake of the horse we lost the battle, for the sake of the battle we lost the war' type situation.

Stick to your awesome purpose

Handle setbacks objectively. All too many businesses rationalise setbacks. They interpret the setback in the way that confirms their working assumptions about the strategy and the commercial environment they are in. **Don't!** Find out what caused the setback, if it is economical to do so. When is it smart to do so? If you are going to be ploughing in more resources.

Exercise: What have we missed? What other things do you need to do to make sure your strategy works?

THE STRATEGY MONITORING AND IMPROVEMENT GROUP

So now you have a strategy in place and working successfully. The most successful strategies, by definition, are those that are most in tune with customer needs today. To ensure your strategies continue to be in tune with customer needs tomorrow, you need some mental tools to model the current marketplace. I have already suggested that the Four-layer Strategy Model can be used for that purpose. But whatever tools you use to monitor the marketplace, you also must use some kind of ongoing system to gather information from customers, some system to process that information, some system to enable that information to fine-tune the strategy – to tweak the major objectives, objectives, tactics and operating methods until you come up with an even more awesome benefit. Incrementalism has its limits.

That system must take place in some context, in some structure. We have already seen that, in most companies, there is no effective way to revise and review strategy. So what can be done? Form a group which will hold regular Strategy Monitoring and Improvement (SMI) meetings. The SMI group must be made up of the independent thinkers on the board, the non-executive directors. Why? What kind of kind of monitoring of the strategy do you think you would see if those who came up with the strategy were sitting on the SMI group along with those charged with its implementation? Partial or impartial? Objective or self-serving?

So what should your SMI group do? Oversee the gathering of information which will be used to assess the strategy; establish the criteria which will be used to assess the strategy; design the process to gather the information to assess the strategy, and inform the board of all its findings.

How often should the SMI group meet? Bad question. Better question: when will the SMI group have something to do (note the objectives-driven versus ritual-driven distinction)? As often as it takes to make the current strategy redundant. If you do not make your strategy redundant, your competitors will. The SMI group should be seeking ways to improve the strategy. It should be looking for ways to deliver an ever more awesome benefit to the customer. If it does not, your competitors will.

Your strategy should keep the company ahead of emerging competitor offers. It should seek ways to harness new technology to deliver the awesome benefit in an even better way, or faster way, or cheaper way (depending on your strategy). In short, the SMI group should be your competitive think tank.

CAUTION 1

The SMI group should not slip into a situation where the strategic director or manager becomes an honorary member of the group. S/he has too much of an interest in defending the status quo, and the meetings will slip into one long defence by the implementer against the attacks of the thinkers. The SMI group is there to change the status quo, and cannot be staffed by those whose role it is to defend it.

The information for the SMI group must be gathered by outsiders. Why? They have no interest in presenting themselves as being effective presenters of the board's current strategy.

CAUTION 2

The outsiders gathering the information must not report to the managers on whose strategy the information is being gathered. They must *only* report to the SMI group. Neither should the recruitment of the information-gatherers be left to the managers. It must be handled by the SMI group: s/he who hires the piper calls the tune.

This is not a book on strategy, so we will leave the SMI group at this point. But one last issue: could you pull together a sufficient number of independent thinkers to form the SMI group? How many truly independent non-executive directors do you have? If the answer is 'few' or 'none' (as is usual), what price do you pay for that? If the answer is 'few', who can be relied on to ask the awkward questions, the probing questions, the questions that make people think? Get them on your SMI group and even your board, ASAP.

Exercise: What system and structure will you put in place to assess and improve your strategy?

GETTING IT WRONG, GETTING IT RIGHT

The big vacuum cleaner companies all turned down the offer to manufacture the famous Dyson on the grounds that it would mean they would deprive themselves of the lucrative after-sales parts and bags market. Can you believe it? They turned down an awesome benefit in the marketplace on the grounds that their after-sales market would be detrimentally affected. What does this tell us? Well, when you evaluate a potential strategy, by far the most important factor to consider is: 'Will this give us an awesome benefit? Will it enable us to provide some benefit that no one else can offer?' If it does, you will end up being the leader in the field you improve. If it does not . . . someone has to be an also-ran.

What happened after the big manufacturers turned Dyson down? He went on to manufacture the machines himself, and has been an international success. He has made a clean sweep and wiped the floor (sorry, I could not resist it) with the people who previously had the chance to manufacture his product.

After realising its mistake, one company, Hoover, tried to defend itself against the sale of the clearly superior Dyson by promising huge numbers of free flights to people buying their product. They failed to deliver on their apparent promises. There was a national outcry. The name of that company will for a long time be associated with perceived broken promises and the 'free flights scandal'.

Other companies have experienced considerable downturns in their fortunes. Still others have reverse-engineered clones of the Dyson and are now trying to compete. Too late. They will for many, many years be seen as Dyson clones. All because they thought it would affect their after-sales markets. Instead, turning it down affected their entire market; somebody else now has it.

So when evaluating strategy, one of the most important factors, if not the most

important, is: does it deliver an awesome benefit? Does it enable you to deliver a benefit that no one else can offer. If it does and you reject it, beware: there are plenty of Dysons just waiting to wipe you out.

SUMMARY

Strategy-formation is easy for companies that have put the work into creating an awesome purpose, and difficult for those that have not. Predicting the future has always been much harder than making it. Companies devoid of awesome purpose seek to predict the future. Those with awesome purpose commit themselves to making the future. Those who make the future make the rules. Those who try to predict the future end up following the rules. Which group would you rather be in? The choice is yours.

PART SUMMARY

In the same way that you will gradually shape a vision or awesome purpose, you should seek to complete the CAM. Bit by bit, day by day, you will come closer to the complete CAM as you consult and interact with your colleagues, as you suggest and collect ideas.

Part III
Implementation

Now that we have covered the background to and the models of corporate alignment, we are ready to start covering implementation. If you are an experienced business person, you can probably skip Chapter 9 on problems preventing alignment and/or change (indeed, all readers may choose to omit this chapter unless they are faced with obstacles to change which they can't quite pinpoint, otherwise the chapter may feel demotivating). But please do not underestimate the need to be able to pinpoint the cause of the problems thwarting your culture-change efforts. Most successful culture-change projects comprise solving one difficult-to-identify barrier after another.

If you are CEO of your company and you have been completing the exercises as we have gone along, you may find that the first stages of the 9R Model repeat work you have already done. If that is so, please bear with me: the 9R Model simply recounts the stages of effective culture change from start to finish. It had to be included as a complete model for those who are not CEOs and need to know how to effect or trigger change from within an organisation's hierarchy.

9 Overcoming problems that prevent alignment or change

CHAPTER OVERVIEW

- Whole-culture problems
- Purpose problems
- People problems
- Process buy-in problems
- Planning problems
- Performance problems
- Presentation problems
- Examples of resistance to change and its consequences
- Summary

Many factors make change and alignment very difficult in most companies and organisations. If you are going to successfully align or change an organisational culture, you obviously need to know where the barriers are and have some idea of how to cope with them.

WHOLE-CULTURE PROBLEMS

MORIBUND ORGANISATIONS

Sometimes the only way to achieve change with really moribund organisations (take a moment to think of a few) is to have an enormous crisis that threatens the very survival of the organisation (and now take a moment to imagine what crisis would trigger some action in those organisations) and triggers some realisation that change is needed. But do not assume that such crises will automatically trigger the desire to change, or that people will do what is required in order to change the organisation.

Exercise: Think about all of the organisations with which you deal. Which of them could be considered moribund? What is it about them that signals their moribundity? To what extent are those signals also present in your organisation?

We won't change, and you can't make us!

Some organisations seem to be prepared to collapse rather than change their ways. If you are in such an organisation and are not in a position to change it, you would be wise to consider getting out before the collapse happens, for two reasons. First, once the collapse has happened and hits the newspapers, locally or nationally, the fact that that company/organisation name appears on your CV will not help your search for a job. Second, if it is as resistant to change as we have described, your attempts (unless you are in one of the top jobs) to change it, or simply to make people aware that change is necessary, will be construed as disruptive behaviour. You may find yourself isolated or even removed at a time not most convenient to you. So consider this: is it worth flogging a dead horse, or should you abandon it and find one at least capable of a good canter?

Exercise: How moribund would your organisation have to be to encourage you to think that it is time to look elsewhere before the roof caves in?

The situation above is exactly that which leads to bright, talented people joining and, pretty immediately, leaving moribund organisations. Revolving-door companies are not just those which make revolving doors. Mortuaries are not the only places that store dead bodies prior to burial.

Fortunately, most organisations are not staffed by zombies. Fortunately, most people are alive enough to realise that significant threats require significant responses; that a significant threat may put their job and even their pension at risk if they don't become part of the solution.

The less choice people have about the need for change, the more they will embrace the available change options.

TRADITION AND RESISTANCE

The more deeply a culture is steeped in tradition, the more resistant to change it is. In the nineteenth century, Britain was reliant on steam power, as was every other major developed economy. Then along came electric power. Britain was so resistant to change that it lost most of its iron and steel industry to the USA and Germany. What was left of it was taken out in the mid-twentieth century by resistance to change to the flexible working practices prevalent in other parts of the world. Two periods of resistance to change spelled the end of a world-leading industry. How many do you think it would take to kill your company?

In case you thought the above reluctance to change was isolated to Britain, it was not. Unfortunately, Britain has a rather good track record at impeding progress. In 1929, Frank Whittle invented the jet engine. He approached the British government, and his idea was promptly dismissed as 'impractical'. Despite repeated attempts over eight years to persuade those in authority of the merit and potential commercial and military benefits of his invention, still they refused to build a prototype.

Can you imagine it – the greatest advance in flight technology since flight itself being treated in such a way? An invention that would have given Britain world dominance in jet-propulsion technology blocked by petty bureaucrats who would not recognise a good idea if it demonstrated itself to them (as the jet engine did!).

Under what circumstances was the jet engine eventually adopted in Britain? Word leaked out that Germany had developed the engine and had built a prototype aircraft. We could go through virtually every industry and pick out similar examples. The great irony is that Britain is by far the greatest producer of new ideas, most of which fail to raise funding in Britain, and are subsequently funded and exploited abroad. If it was not so sad, it would be funny. If it was not provable fact, you would say it had to be fiction.

CATASTROPHIC SHOCK

It often takes a catastrophic shock to knock a culture out of its complacency. Both Japan and Germany have reached the top of the world economic rankings since their total and catastrophic defeats in the Second World War. Other countries not so shaken seem not to have fared so well – Italy and Britain, for instance. Britain in particular suffered the most devastating of diseases: complacency. It is most often caused by success and affluence. One of the worst things that could happen to your company is for it to become extremely successful and cash-rich very quickly. It would breed such complacency that you would be unlikely to achieve anything ever again. Only by playing down the success and making your staff aware of the looming threats of competitors and others are you likely to be able to keep complacency at bay.

UNCOMFORTABLE RIPPLES

Frequently, a culture will resist a change, not because it is a bad idea, not because the benefits are not as promised, but because of the side-effects the change will bring about. The disruption to the other elements of the culture may be too great in the minds of the constituents. That was the scenario when Galileo presented his evidence.

Exercise: When have you seen good ideas that would have been of enormous benefit to an organisation rejected because of the discomfort the ripples from the change would have caused? What happened to that organisation's place in the market?

CULTURE/MINI-CULTURE CONFUSION

All too often I have seen a situation in which the directors and senior managers have their own culture. When asked to describe the company culture, they describe their own mini-culture, not the culture of the company, which is often very, very different.

If the directors of a company do not know what its real culture is, how can they manage it? How can they change it? How can they harness it? How can they align it?

CULTURE-DENIAL

What is worse than not knowing what a culture actually is? Denying what a culture actually is. Most senior managers and directors like to think that they have a progressive, dynamic business culture which harnesses the best in all their staff, just as 98 per cent of all drivers think their driving standard is above average. Even in the face of incontrovertable evidence, many company managers will claim they have culture *y* when patently they have culture *x*. No change is possible under those circumstances. Until the reality of the culture is acknowledged, no positive change will take place. Any change attempts based on the mistaken view of the culture will result in quite a bit of damage.

MACHIAVELLIAN PROBLEMS

Political in-fighting and inter-fiefdom rivalries

If you are in a culture where position is more important than performance, you will find that few people are prepared to accept changes for fear of weakening their position.

A strong blame element exists in the current culture. In cultures where there must always be a culprit for anything that has gone wrong, you will see strong resistance to taking any decisions or making any changes. Who wants to make change if they are liable to be blamed if it does not go exactly to plan (as is the case with most change)?

Low ethical standards/lack of trust

Success is *always* based on trust. If you have some managers whose track record is one of undermining others, stabbing their 'enemies' in the back and conning their staff, you can forget about them being successful change-managers. In organisations where duplicity and deceit are seen as acceptable ways to behave, change will be extremely difficult. People will assume that they are being set up for something. They will trust no one and nothing, so change will be nearly impossible.

On the other hand, if you have managers who genuinely care for their people, keep their word, never blame anyone else for their mistakes, behave as though they care for the future of the organisation, involve their people in decision-making and empower their staff to work within agreed frameworks, then you probably have several potentially good change-managers.

Only management are paid to think

How often have you seen it? Bright members of staff put forward ideas to help the company, and they are rejected or ignored. They are rejected on the grounds that since it is the management's job to think and the person putting forward the idea is not in a 'thinking job', the idea cannot possibly be of any merit. They obviously cannot be in command of all the facts necessary to make sensible suggestions. Take that attitude a few times, and what happens?

ALOOFNESS WITH AND DISTANCE FROM THE CUSTOMER

Many companies are not in touch with their customers. The company becomes more interested in internal processes than in external outcomes. If you are not in touch with the customer, how can you possibly know what they want you to change? If you do not know what they want you to change, how can you change to make sure you keep their business? If you do not change while everyone else around you does, what will happen? No customers. If you start losing customers, whose fault is it? Is it your competitors' fault for offering better products or services? Or is it your fault for having been aloof?

Exercise: Name five organisations that you know of which seem to be aloof or out of touch with their customers?

DRASTIC ACTION AGAINST ENTRENCHED RESISTANCE

When a destructive and doomed culture is so embedded that all reasonable attempts fail to change it, more dramatic action may be required. You may remember how Rupert Murdoch created a new culture in one of his newspaper businesses.

The Fleet Street-based printers were refusing to change and use new methods and technology. Despite protracted and extensive negotiations, the staff refused to budge. Solution: build a new facility, recruit new staff into a newly created culture, and shut down the old unit. It was a resounding success. Rupert Murdoch is now the world leader in his field.

Exercise: What do you currently do in your organisation when someone refuses to make a reasonable change for the benefit of the company? If your answer does not include some reference to dismissal, what signal are you sending out to the whole organisation about how they can treat change initiatives?

PURPOSE PROBLEMS

INSUFFICIENTLY BIG 'WHY'

Another major reason for failure in culture change is that people do not really know where they are being taken, and why. As Nietzsche nearly said: 'Give people a strong enough "why" and they can tolerate almost any "how".' This has been proven over and over again. The CEOs with the greatest scope to effect changes are those who are looking over into the abyss at a bankruptcy situation. That gives the staff a pretty strong 'why' to change. If a less powerful 'why' is in place, more 'how' information is required. Staff want to know how you propose to get between here and now, and there and then, and how it will affect them.

Exercise: How is this barrier to change addressed by an awesome purpose?

LACK OF CLEAR OBJECTIVES

Culture change will definitely fail if top management do not spell out a clear picture of what the organisation will look like after the change. Obviously, implicit in that are the assumptions that good and consistent communication is required, and that people will be trained to do that which they are required to do in order to make the change successful. The number of times managers simply do not think about doing these things is staggering. Please make sure you do.

Things are OK around here. There is no problem.

Denial is easy when the problem is not in your face. Denial is easy when you pick up a great salary, drive a prestige car and live in an impressive house. Denial is easy until the problems are undeniable. Then it is too late. Goodbye, nice car; great to have known you, salary; see you again some day, house. (More on this later.)

OK FOR BIG PLAYERS

In the conferences and seminars I present, one objection to these ideas that regularly horrifies me is: 'That's OK for the big successful multinational companies. We are just a medium-sized national; we don't have the resources to do those things.' I can remember not a single conference or public seminar for any group at any level in which someone has not uttered those words, or ones very close to them (other than conferences and seminars for the big multinationals, obviously). A few people just do not get it. The reason those companies are huge international successes is because they use those methods. In the majority of cases, they have used the methods for a very, very long time. They do not use the methods because they are big multinationals; they are big multinationals because they use the methods.

If you are reading this book after attending the Awesome Purpose Seminar, can you remember the location in the hall/room of the person who raised the objection, and the phrasing they used?

POOR UNDERSTANDING OF THE NEED FOR VISION, MISSION OR AWESOME PURPOSE

Some managers just don't appreciate how inspiring a vision can be. Perhaps they assume that because they have dull, going-nowhere lives of quiet desperation, everybody else is like that too. They are not. Most people crave for a bigger and longer-lasting cause than themselves. Most people will perform at superior levels given a powerful vision: an awesome purpose.

VISION-VARIATION AND MISSION DRIFT

Mission drift is characterised by: today all your staff understand exactly where there are going; tomorrow it will be slightly changed, and the day after that it will have changed again. Result: staff have no clear or fixed vision, although it may appear, in snapshot, that the organisation does have a vision. You must be consistent in your awesome purpose.

Exercise: When have you seen mission drift at work? What effect did it have on the focus of the organisation? What effect did it have on the decision-making abilities of the staff?

PARALYSIS BY ANALYSIS

Even companies with stable and inspiring visions can, in effect, have no vision if they overdo the analysis. If each time a decision has to be taken, a full analysis has to be conducted, you soon find a situation where you have a backlog of decisions, each dependent on the next. Result: paralysis by analysis.

People who make decisions quickly with the available information usually find this situation difficult to imagine. But it is a very real barrier to change in many organisations. It usually occurs where there are very tight reporting requirements, and where the work conducted is highly analytical and calculation-based.

141

Exercise: Which departments in your organisation seem to get bogged down in analysis? What type of resistance to change do you think you will see from that department?

MINIMAL RETURN

Many cynics claim that pursuing some kind of unifying goal will take years to produce any serious return. Well, let's see.

If the mere existence of a clear goal increased overall staff productivity by just 1 per cent, would you be interested? If a shared vision reduced the amount of in-fighting and consequently increased co-operation by just 1 per cent, would you be interested? If the existence of any awesome purpose which people believed in increased people's desire to come to work and subsequently reduced absenteeism by 1 per cent, would you be interested? If the ideas that staff generated in order to help you achieve the awesome purpose increased operating efficiency by just 1 per cent, would you be interested?

We've just increased your profit margin by a considerable amount, and we

haven't spent a penny – and we're still years from achieving the awesome purpose. So the question is: do the cynics have the future, or will you?

PEOPLE PROBLEMS

The following are players in the game of change:

- resisters
- promoters
- fence-sitters

The more change-promoters you have, the faster the change will be, and the more effective it will be once achieved. The fence-sitters won't move until the change looks as though it will work. Even the resisters will play along when they can actually see the evidence that the change is working, and that it will be permanent.

HOW TO GET THE RESISTERS AND FENCE-SITTERS ON BOARD

As I have said before: when you put the same facts before most rational people, they will come to the same conclusions, assuming that they have the same values and agenda – to make the company's future more secure and more prosperous. When people are drawing different conclusions from the same facts, their values and/or agendas are different, and that is made clear to all. This is yet another reason why it pays to have an agreed and shared set of values in any organisation.

HANDLING RESISTERS

It *always* pays to listen to people who are raising objections to plans. If they have raised an objection, they obviously feel strongly enough to stand up and be counted. That means they are committed to achieving something. If you can get them to express the objective behind their concerns by asking questions and listening to them, you may find that they will, in turn, be more inclined to listen to you. If you want to create a corporate terrorist, just blank them out. Like all terrorists, they will rarely reveal themselves, but will cause a huge amount of hit-and-run damage when you least need it, when you can least afford it.

Exercise: Why do you think blanking people causes such resentment? If you have difficulty answering that question, think about how you felt when a superior last blanked you.

Having listened, you will frequently find that you are both trying to achieve the

143

same end but have slightly different views about how to achieve it. Different opinions, even though the agenda is the same, almost always reflect different values. If that is so, you have a chance to find the value basis for the different opinions. Once you have found the different value at work behind the objection, you then know what you have to work on – either by getting the individual to audit the company values, or to strengthen the role of the company values in decision-making.

CHANGE-HYPOCRISY

Change is the force that brought us to the high standard of living which we have today. It brought us from bare feet to shoes, to the horse and cart, on to the steam train, on to the car. Change took us into the air, from balloons to propeller-driven planes, on to jet aircraft and eventually to the moon. Change took us from caves, to lean-tos, on to huts, and on to stone houses and beyond. Change took us from sticking our heads in streams and ponds, to buckets in the local pool or stream, to running hot and cold water in every home. Change took us from darkness to fire, on to candles, and on to the light bulb in all its current varieties.

Change-hypocrisy

We could fill the rest of this book doing nothing more than listing the sequence of changes that each of us benefits from in the many different areas of our lives. Yet a huge number of people resist change. They lap up the benefits of millions of changes, yet try to prevent change. What drives such bizarre behaviour? Fear of the unknown. Before the change, they knew the rules of the game, but after . . .? How do you deal with that? Make sure they know the rules of the game that will be played after the change. Better still, get them involved in planning the change and therefore setting the rules for their post-change world.

Exercise: When you were in more junior positions, what was the thing you most wanted to know about changes?

GETTING PEOPLE TO OWN CHANGE

Let us look at ownership, first from the point of view of what makes people feel deprived of ownership and what effects that has on them. People fear the unknown. It is maybe the most frightening of all the things. Why? Our imagination conjures up all sorts of monstrous scenarios, if we let it. What triggers that? Two things: lack of control and lack of knowledge. People deprived of knowledge and control over changes that affect them will be fearful of the change. That fear will trigger defensiveness or aggressiveness. By thinking about what knowledge and control the affected people will want, we can make their co-operation more likely, or at the very least, their resistance less likely.

Knowledge of the change falls into two categories: that which is known; that which is not known or is unknowable, but will become known in time. If staff are told everything that is known and that which is not known (genuinely not known), their fear of the unknown is reduced, and this enables them to cope better with change.

Control falls into three categories: that which you can control; that which you can't control but can influence; that which you can neither influence nor control. Showing people what they can control and influence empowers them, and thus enables them to cope better with change.

How do you get that control? By asking people what they can do or offer in order to help the desired change. That way people have influence and/or control over the way the change will affect them.

BLOCKING REFRAMING

You might have to read the introduction to the reframing section (see pages 180–208) to make sense of what follows. Some very bright individuals may foresee the consquences of reframing and seek to block that redefinition of the problem in order to avoid those consequences – even if that is the right thing for the organisation.

POOR CHANGE-LEADERSHIP

Can you imagine anyone trying to lead a culture-change or alignment programme who has no understanding of the sequence of events required to reach the end result? Of course not. Yet, as above, many managers are put in charge of change programmes and not given the kind of training they ought to have in order to bring them up to speed.

THEORY–REALITY MISMATCH

Many people who co-operate with the proposed changes at the planning stage become resistant at the implementation stage. The reality of the changes suddenly hits them, and they start digging in their heels.

PERSONAL BARRIERS

Pressure from the friends of each staff member is a serious barrier to change. Each friend has their own reasons for wishing the person concerned to stay as they are. Your organisation and all staff may be in a changing world, but to their friends and relatives that one person is the only thing that is changing. One person in the family or friendship circle is changing and trying to upset the apple cart. Their friends will act to keep the cart stable. The person changing has to find a way of doing so that satisfies his or her stakeholders in the same way that the company seeking the change has to satisfy its stakeholders.

How does that manifest itself? Usually in the form of experimentation. The person concerned will explore new behaviours to see which are most rewarded by their environment. Those behaviours which are resisted by either group will disappear quickly. Those which are most rewarded by both groups will stay.

Exercise: When was the last time you complained that someone was not the way they used to be? What did you do to encourage the re-emergence of the person you once knew?

RULE-RIGIDITY

Some people love rules and logical procedures – in fact, they are totally lost without them. Rules are their signposts and walking sticks. Remove them or change them and you are threatening an entire way of life. The only way to help these people is to provide a new set of rules before the old ones are discarded. The CAM, implemented properly, does exactly that.

WE'RE TOO BUSY TRYING TO STAY AFLOAT TO WORRY ABOUT CHANGE: EMOTIONAL EXCESS

For those who handle life's problems by going into an emotional tailspin, the prospect of significant organisational change will put them into every aviator's nightmare: an inverted tailspin. How do you handle those people? How do you handle those who seem to take great pleasure in upsetting displays of emotions?

Inverted emotional tailspin

Having completed the CAM with their input, your next step is to acknowledge to them that they have a problem. Then help them come up with some way of coping with the change.

Exercise: Find five reasons to justify parting with some cash for such a stunningly wonderful investment as finding a way to help staff cope with the change.

PROCESS PROBLEMS

It's too difficult.

Don't laugh. It *is* difficult; coming up with an awesome purpose is extremely difficult. The apparently simple objective of getting an organisation to distil and adopt a shared vision is extremely tough. That is why so few businesses have a clear vision. Those companies which have found an awesome purpose persevered in doing so knowing that they would gain an incredible advantage over those who would give up 'because it's too difficult'.

KILL THE PAIN, IGNORE THE CAUSE

How often have you seen it? There is some big problem in a company. Someone promoted beyond the level of their competence 'knows' how to deal with it. They put in place a great pain-killing process, but unfortunately, because the cause is still in place doing damage (undetected because of the pain-killer), the problem starts to have knock-on effects elsewhere, and before you know it you have blood poisoning when previously you just had toothache.

Whatever change-management process you use, it must address the cause of the problem. Setting up a process to deal with the symptoms only makes things worse in the long run.

TREATMENTS CLASHING WITH CULTURE

If you try solving a problem with a process incompatible with your culture, you are unlikely to be successful. Trying such a thing will not only fail to produce results, it will reduce the clarity with which people see their culture. Your failed treatment will have sent cultural signals in the same way any other management decision sends signals. Let's look at this in a bit more detail.

INITIATIVE MISMATCH

Yet another reason change initiatives often fail (it's almost fashionable to have pieces of failed initiatives cluttering company boardrooms) is that they simply do not match the profile of the company.

When, oh when will companies realise that the latest snake-oil initiatives simply do not deliver in the vast majority of cases? When, oh when will they realise that having everyone pointing in the same direction is more powerful than all the re-engineering, JIT, MRP, TQM, blah, blah, blah put together?

Exercise: How many initiatives has your company introduced in the last five years? How many of them have increased profitability by as little as 10 per cent? None? OK, let's move down a level. How many of them have produced greater returns than they cost? A few? Any? How many of them were successfully implemented, even if they cost more than they delivered? One? Two? None?

PROCESS BUY-IN PROBLEMS

The people who were happy with MBO (Management By Objectives) and resisted 'mission statements' are still around. Most have only bought into the need to have mission statements in the last five to ten years. But we've moved on. We now know the concept of mission is too simple to be effective. Yes, it's better than MBO, and it is much better than nothing at all, but it's still not good

Boardroom failures

enough. Unfortunately, persuading your resident cynics of that takes thought, time and effort.

Exercise: Who is your best resident cynic? Ask them to prepare a list of why the proposed changes won't and can't work. Use that list, in addition to the barriers presented in this chapter, to prepare yourself to handle the objections offered by those you have to persuade of the need for change.

RESISTANCE TO CHANGE IS DESIGNED IN

Most companies are set up to prevent anything other than what was intended to happen from happening. The very processes, structures and systems that most need to change are the things that are best equipped, best designed to resist change.

Exercise: Test that hypothesis. Ask your managers what happens to anything or anyone who steps outside of the established system. You'll hear some ingenious ways of stifling change. Take a note of those; they will have to be addressed if your change or alignment initiative is to succeed.

NO SYSTEM TO SPOT ENVIRONMENTAL CHANGES

You will know from your own company that there is usually no one appointed to monitor the commercial environment. There is usually no SMI group (see pages 126–128). If a company does not have an eye on the changes taking place in the commercial environment, how can it possibly hope to respond to them? It can't.

PLANNING PROBLEMS

SOME POOR PLANNING ON THE CHANGE FRONT

Change for its own sake? Change should always be aimed at increasing performance. Even change introduced to help the company become more change-tolerant should be aimed primarily at some performance improvement.

Accommodating the need for involvement must not overwhelm profit-production. Giving some people too much involvement invites them to put up every conceivable barrier to change. For most people, the more they are involved, the more they will go beyond mere co-operation and move towards initiation.

It is vital to choose the behaviour and approach that is most effective for each task. Habitually using the same approach to all change situations will not achieve change. You must be flexible with your approaches to change.

Avoid giving and taking too little initiative/empowerment. The change process is so complex and multi-faceted that you cannot expect to report on your every decision and action. Your staff would be in and out of your office all day. That is yet another reason you should have a clear set of values and an awesome purpose.

SOME POOR BELIEFS ABOUT ALIGNMENT AND CHANGE-MANAGEMENT

- A strong clique of top-rate staff can push change through.
- Mistakes are the end of your career rise.
- Get to the top for security and easy money.
- Make all key decisions yourself.
- Telling people what to do is the basis of good change-management.

Of course, the opposite of each of these is what is actually required.

No team can drive change without the consent of the constituents of a culture. All staff should be involved. Being willing to make mistakes is the only way to get experience. Delegate as much of the decision-making as you can – the people most committed to implementing decisions successfully are those who take them. Asking people what to do is the basis of good performance. Being someone who gets results is the most sure ticket to security and good money.

PILOT TESTS

Many companies are tempted to pilot their culture change in some small department. Sounds commercially prudent, does it not? Test on a small scale before you sign up for the full thing.

So why does it fail? Perhaps a scenario will make it clear. Imagine you speak 'Gramset' (a made-up language) and practise Woodbrille (a made-up religion).

A small group of you are placed in the middle of any major city and told to carry on business in the same way as the group you are replacing. The previous group spoke the local language and practised the majority religion. Are you going to fit into the prevailing culture? Are you going to be able to conduct business effectively? Of course not. Yes, you would integrate eventually, but how long is eventually? Would you have no problems with the majority groupings? No, you would have many. A change has been imposed on them – you. They won't like it. They don't speak Gramset and are frightened by this new Woodbrille religion. They don't understand the strange practices it involves.

OK, so it is an example taken to extremes for the purposes of illustration. But that is exactly the scenario you would create if you tried a pilot culture-change experiment. Can you imagine the confusion if one link in your value chain had a different culture from the others?

However, do not take that to mean that you should change your entire culture all in one fell swoop either. Not a good idea. What it means is that culture change is gradual and covers the whole organisation simultaneously.

Exceptions exist to most rules. If you are setting up a new company or a new division within a company that will be autonomous, it should be allowed to have its own independent culture. In fact, that may be a way of proving that an alternative culture can be made to work as part of your organisation.

UNFAIR REWARDS

How do you react when you have been slogging away to effect an important change, while witnessing one of your 'colleagues' doing their utmost to resist your changes, or even sabotaging them. Then when your change succeeds, your 'colleague' proclaims how much of a contribution they made to the change and is then rewarded by top management. How is that going to affect your faith in the judgement of top management? Obvious, really. Could such a thing happen? Yes, simply because top management do not get involved with their staff. They are so distant that they don't know who is pulling the wool over their eyes. But the other staff do, and that knowledge of how senior managers treat those who really do the work will detrimentally affect the credibility of senior management.

CREEPING INFLEXIBILITY

As sure as night follows day, dynamic and flexible companies slowly, gradually, eventually become inflexible. How? The people who understand culture and thus manage it well are replaced, as they retire or move on to fry bigger fish, by people whose understanding of culture is limited – or worse, by people who

Maintain cultural flexibility or . . .

think culture equals control systems. Before long, a world-leading company is facing bankruptcy.

NO SYSTEM TO MAINTAIN CULTURE-FLEXIBILITY

There is always a tension between absence of system and too rigorous a system. The opposite of the above barrier is also a barrier – the absence of a system to manage culture. It sounds strange to say that you need a system to manage flexibility, but you do. If you don't have one, your culture will lose its flexibility, or become so flexible that it falls apart.

PERFORMANCE PROBLEMS

WHY MOST CULTURE-CHANGE PROGRAMMES FAIL

The biggest and most common reason for the failure of virtually all culture-change programmes is poor leadership, usually caused by lack of understanding of culture and its components.

Ignorance of culture

Can you imagine any manager lacking in a general understanding of culture, or a specific understanding of the culture that they are trying to change, being successful in their attempts to do so? Of course not. How could anyone hope to succeed under such circumstances? Yet daily, all over the world, people are trying to do exactly that.

If you insist on getting an internal person to conduct your culture-change programme, please make sure they understand culture and culture change before you let them loose on the company. Naturally – again with total impartiality – I can recommend a rather good seminar on the subject: the Awesome Purpose Seminar! (Write to me at the address given in the Preface if you are interested.)

Benchmark resistance

In my work, I regularly come up against the cynics. Indeed, most of the barriers to change mentioned in this book have come straight from their mouths. They say: 'There is no point in comparing ourselves to these cultural benchmarks you have set; we will never reach them.' Probably true. But who will be in a stronger position, you or a company which is much closer to measuring up to the cultural alignment benchmarks (see pages 231–232)? Obviously, those who are closer. Clearly, striving towards the ideal is worthwhile. Remember this: the ideal beyond reach today is the entry level of tomorrow. Whoever writes the equivalent of *Awesome Purpose* in twenty years' time will look back and wonder why such basic cultural alignment standards were thought to be at the cutting edge. Cultural alignment at the standard advocated is the smart, competitive option; but it won't be for long.

Exercise: So far, we have laid out the cumulative best in cultural alignment. Go a stage further: what would the idealised benchmarks in the perfectly aligned company look like?

'Brilliant, but . . .'

People hate making mistakes, particularly in a culture which promotes those who make no mistakes. Such a promotion policy sends out powerful and highly destructive messages. It says: 'Take no risks for the company's benefit, make no stances, never try to achieve anything not certain of success which is not backed by everyone and their next-door neighbour's dog.'

Before long you have a culture headed for the corporate graveyard. Companies that fail to innovate fail, period. How? Why? A thousand and one reasons are available to kill any good idea. Everything is 'brilliant, but . . .'. How do you deal with this? Show them the inevitable consequences of changing nothing. Start promoting those who do take well thought-out risks (see the second edition of *Opportunity Spotting*, MacLennan 1998, for more details). Start rewarding those who make changes.

If all else fails, get heavy. Use your legal right as a company manager to manage the company. Issue the necessary directives, set the necessary objectives, and if they are not met, take the necessary disciplinary action. Although a manager's right to manage is enshrined in the laws of most countries, you may have some legal hurdles to pass through before you can justify sacking those who do not carry out the change directives. But as I said, this is absolutely the last resort. If you do not take this action, your staff will note that you will tolerate non-co-operation with change directives. Those who are so inclined will take that as a strong signal that they can ignore all subsequent change directives.

Exercise: Check that you are fully aware of what employment law in your country requires you to do before you dismiss those who fail to comply with change objectives.

Busy fools

The way to put things right is to work harder.

Of course not! What is required is not harder work, but smarter work. What we are talking about here is the difference between doing things right and doing the right thing. Busy fools deal with need for change by working harder. In other words, they continue to do more of the wrong things right. Instead of

helping the situation, they often make it even worse. What they need to do correctly are the right things.

Initiative fatigue

If your company has a recent history of many initiatives being introduced, you may find that few people have any stomach left for yet another. That will be even more the case if there is a history of one initiative being introduced before the last one has bedded in, and even more true if there have been many failures with the initiatives that have been attempted. Staff will expect yet another failure, and consequently will put little effort into the latest pearl of wisdom from senior management. Your previous organisational performance at change-management (or lack of it) may be the biggest barrier to cultural alignment.

Inappropriate or absent performance measures

Performance measures are often set at too low a level and/or measure entirely inappropriate behaviours. As a result, people have to change little or nothing in order to appear to be meeting the performance targets. Another common performance disaster is that objectives are set on an activity basis, rather than on an outcome basis.

Collective irresponsibility

The big danger with so-called 'collective responsibility' is that it all too often and all too quickly becomes collective irresponsibility. No one in the organisation actually takes responsibility for areas they all apparently share. When the going gets tough, that so-called 'collective responsibility' usually degenerates into a search for someone to blame: 'We are achieving our targets here; you are not achieving your targets there. What are *you* going to do about it?'

Consequently, staff and managers are reluctant to admit to making mistakes. If they do it once, it will be assumed that the next time there is a healthy ration of blame to be distributed, they will be the willing recipients. Everyone else witnesses the way the 'victim' is treated, and resolves not to admit to mistakes or misjudgements. Before long you have a company which never makes mistakes of any kind. A company that never makes mistakes can never make change. To admit to the need for change is to admit to having made mistakes yesterday. Of course, you and I can see that this is patent nonsense, but in the mindset necessary to function in that kind of culture, it is good survival logic.

Exercise: Name the last two occasions on which you were party to a decision you would not have been happy to make on your own.

PRESENTATION PROBLEMS

MERE WORDS

All words! This CAM structure is all about semantics and wordcraft. All good intent and no substance. Visions, values and purposes are mere words.

How do you handle that kind of resistance? Ask these people if they are grateful for the 'mere words' that Churchill uttered to unite the free world against tyranny. Or if they would be afraid of the 'mere words' that Hitler used to unleash the most horrifying atrocity in history.

The CAM *is* about wordcraft. It is about putting into words that which already exists, but is not articulated. It is about putting into words that which must be communicated to get the whole organisation facing in the same direction, or singing from the same song sheet.

Elements of the CAM are just words until they are adopted by those for whom they have meaning. Then, those mere words are turned into action, into behaviour, into the kind of action that takes human beings to the moon. Yes, they are words, but 'mere words'? Most definitely not!

If that does not do it for your resident cynic, ask them what they are railing against? What is it that is making them so aggressively defensive? Yes, that's right: 'mere words' have got them digging their heels in; 'mere words' have aroused their passions; 'mere words' have got under their skin – the same 'mere words' they claimed would have no effect!

COMPLACENCY

Many change programmes fail to shake managers out of their complacency. Why are some managers complacent in the face of evidence that even a high-school business studies student would regard as indicating a screaming need for change? Because the concerns of stakeholders rarely get to the levels of management in a position to make the changes. The information is just not presented to them.

The roof is still on the building, there are no earthquakes, there is no sign of any crisis. What is your problem?

That is what you might hear if you raise a problem in the face of complacency. Most businesses die slowly from sub-symptomatic illnesses, until, of course, the disease is so widespread that the end is quick and unexpected.

With profits increasing by 5 per cent per year, there can be no problem, right? Wrong. If everyone else in the industry is increasing their profits by 25 per cent, you have big problems. If their market share is increasing at your expense, you had better wake up and smell the coffee before you wake up and smell the liquidator.

FINANCIAL BOREDOM

How often have you been in a board meeting and seen the financial report or budget passed in two or three minutes when a one-hour debate on what to call the new departments has just preceded it? It seems many managers just do not attend to the financial side of the organisation.

You must zap people out of their complacency if there is to be any chance of dealing with the emergent problem. No crisis, no change. No change may mean no company. Most change initiatives fail at the first hurdle: too few people think there is a real problem.

Surrounded by the trappings of executive wealth, it is difficult to convince yourself that you are going down the tubes. So how can you shake managers out of their complacency?

- Remove the trappings of wealth.
- Set targets that can only be achieved if people change.
- Set outcome measures, and use them.
- Expose managers to customers and other stakeholders regularly.
- Expose managers to the problems of the organisation. People need to know what is going wrong before they can put it right.

You may have to 'engineer' a situation in which problems are, shall we say, 'highlighted' in order to get a crisis atmosphere going. I'm not suggesting a fabrication, rather an emphasis on the problems of the organisation.

EXAMPLES OF RESISTANCE TO CHANGE AND ITS CONSEQUENCES

Direct Line (a UK insurance company) slashed the costs of insurance by cutting out the middle man (the broker). It took the rest of the insurance industry seven to ten years to start competing with them, despite the huge market share they took virtually overnight. Why did it take the industry so long to respond? The insurance culture is one which is highly resistant to change, even when the advantages of change are broadcast on national TV and radio every week for nearly ten years (as was the case with the Direct Line advertising campaign). It begs the question: what on earth were the strategic people and directors of the other insurance companies doing in the face of such well-publicised competition? For the vast majority, the sad answer is 'Nothing.' And the sad reason: they were and are rigid cultures.

In the last few years we have seen some of the reactive cultures actually stirring from their slumber to offer their own direct products. What are they offering? Copy-cat products. How does that position them in the market? Also-rans; Johnny-come-latelies, and everybody can see it. Are these companies reacting or responding? Clearly, reacting.

Other companies have seen the power of the direct approach and have applied it to areas that had hitherto escaped Direct Line. Virgin applied it to the pensions and PEP markets (a special tax-free Personal Equity Plan scheme set up by the government to encourage saving). At the time of writing, Virgin are changing the face of that market. Are the companies in that field doing anything about it? Silly question, really. Of course not!

HUBRIS

To those companies praised in this book, and those who are doing the same things and take the praise to also apply to themselves, beware of hubris. Many of the companies praised in recent business books have taken a nosedive. They seem to fall into decline from sitting back on their laurels. They break the cardinal rule: continue seeking ways to provide your customer with more value than anyone else. They stopped pusuing their awesome purpose. By stopping to pat themselves on the back for protracted periods, they gave their competitors time to catch up and overtake them.

INSUFFICIENT EDUCATION AND COMMUNICATION

Probably the cardinal sin in culture change and alignment is a sin of omission rather than commission. Many change attempts fail because they do not communicate the need for change or the method of change sufficiently well, or sufficiently widely, or sufficiently frequently. However much communication you currently think is enough to achieve change, multiply that by ten and you will still be well short of the mark. A successful change programme will take up 60

per cent of all your time for as long as the change is happening, and most of that time will go on communication.

SUMMARY

The constantly changing business environment means that what was an asset yesterday will tomorrow be a liability; good ideas today are burdens tomorrow; leading-edge knowledge of today will reflect poor education tomorrow; premium products of today will be low-cost standards tomorrow.

> *Unless the you of today is constantly seeking to knock the you of yesterday off the top slot, someone else will tomorrow.*

All that good intent will come to nothing if you allow the barriers just discussed to stand between you and a well-aligned and market-responsive or market-creating company. Think of it this way: each barrier you allow to defeat you is yet another nail in your organisation's coffin.

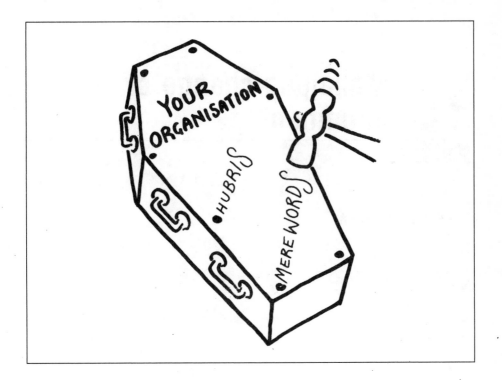

10 Managing change or alignment

CHAPTER OVERVIEW

- The 9R Model
- The 6P Model
- Purpose
- Planning
- Process
- People
- Presentation
- Performance
- Relating the 9 Rs to the 6 Ps

The CAM is a framework to describe, assess and align a culture. To implement the alignment or changes, other supportive tools are needed – the 9R and 6P models. Although both are called 'models', one is the sequence of change steps (9R) and the other is a checklist of factors you will have to consider during each of those steps (6P).

THE 9R MODEL

Most successful outcomes are achieved by following an effective and logical process. The more complex the task, the more systematic a process is required. Alignment and change are no different. Here are the logical steps collectively known as the 9R Model:

1. **Realisation** – reaching a state of awareness that there is a problem
2. **Rallying** – gathering support for the realisation, and spreading it
3. **Recognition** – recognising in full that there is a problem, and getting to the point where enough people acknowledge the problem and what needs to be done to make change/alignment possible

4. **Reframing** – redefining the problem in a way which is in tune with reality
5. **Re-visioning** – completing the CAM, and agreeing an awesome purpose
6. **Redesigning** – designing the systems and structure in line with the CAM that will deliver the awesome purpose
7. **Re-aligning** – implementing the CAM and the redesign
8. **Revising** – evaluating progress, and adjusting the redesign plan as required
9. **Retaining** – working to maintain both the changes and the change-readiness created

We will go into detail in Chapters 11–13, which deal with each of the 9 Rs, so I will leave further explanation until then.

THE 6P MODEL

The 9 Rs form a sequence making up a process to achieve change in the whole organisation. Individual motivation for and co-operation with each phase of change is affected by several elements:

1. **Purpose**
2. **Planning**
3. **Presentation**
4. **Process**
5. **People**
6. **Performance**

The 6 Ps are the factors you must consider at each of the 9 Rs to make them happen successfully.

The purpose of the change, the process used to conduct it, the way the change is presented and communicated, the way the change is planned, who is involved in each of the elements of the change (setting purpose, planning, carrying out the process, and so on) all determine how well that change is/will be implemented. The 6 Ps are the things you need to think about when implementing the 9 Rs, or indeed any other decision you have to implement in your organisation.

To help you become familiar with the the 6P Model and show you how effective it is as a checklist for all management decisions, let's go through each P and present the kinds of questions it is designed to prompt in your mind.

Before we do that, it should be pointed out that none of the 6 Ps operates in isolation. Planning cannot be conducted without reference to process, people, presentation, and so on. The people issues cannot be contemplated without reference to performance, purpose, and so on. In fact, when considering each of the 6 Ps, you also need to consider the subordinate role of each of the other 5 Ps: hence the format of the model (see page 166).

PURPOSE

You have to decide what the purpose of each of the 9 Rs is for you in your context. For example, what are you trying to achieve in the reframing phase or the redesign stage? (Note that 'purpose' here is defined as 'objective', and not in the same way as in the CAM. Yes, I know it's inconsistent, but '5 Ps and an O' just doesn't have the same mnemonic appeal!)

CONSIDERING THE OTHER 5 PS

Then you should give consideration to the other 5 Ps: you should consider the achievement of purpose from the perspective of planning, presentation, process, people and performance.

- Has a plan been drawn up to clarify and communicate the purpose of the change?
- Has the process of agreeing the purpose of the change been established, agreed and communicated?
- How will the purpose of the change and its process be presented?
- Which people will be involved in establishing the purpose of the change?
- Who will perform the tasks involved, and how will that performance be assessed?

A well thought-out purpose will give a crystal-clear 'why', a crystal-clear 'what' and a crystal-clear 'how'.

PLANNING

Whichever of the 9 Rs you are working on during a change programme, you will have to consider how it will be successfully completed. It will have to be planned. Here are just some of the people issues your plan will have to consider:

- How will the staff be given the information which demonstrates the necessity for a programme?
- How will the staff be involved in setting the objectives for solving the problem?
- How will the staff be consulted on the best ways of achieving the objectives?
- How will you ensure staff feel involved in the programme from start to finish?
- How will you communicate what, with whom, and when?

CONSIDERING THE OTHER 5 PS

- How will the performance of the plan be assessed?
- What is the planning process?
- How will the plans be presented?

● What is the purpose of the plan?

PROCESS

You can probably see the pattern by now. The thinking about each P is completed by going through the other 5 Ps. Managing each of the 9 Rs is conducted by thinking of the 6 Ps – purpose, planning, presentation, process, people and performance – you need to establish the purpose for which you are designing a process; consider who will design and carry out the process; plan the process; set performance targets and outcome measures for that process; decide how the need for the process, the call to design it and the completed version of it will be presented. You can see even in the last clause that the other Ps have an influence on how you will present your process.

PEOPLE

Who will plan the changes? Who will carry out the changes (people)? How are those who are required to change being supported (process)? What targets will be set for whom in relation to the planned changes (performance)? Have they been shown how to perform the required changes (presentation)? How will you present the purpose of the changes in the language of each stakeholder group (presentation)? How will your people be informed (presentation) of the change process? How will they be involved in its design (planning)? How are those who are affected by the change being presented with the information? How will change-promoters be publicly and privately valued (presentation)? Have the systems to reward those people co-operating with the changes been set up (process)? In short, the other 5 Ps must be considered when considering the people aspects of each of the 9 Rs.

PRESENTATION

To whom will what be presented? How will the presentation of information be planned, and by whom? What process will be used to get regular information out to those who need it? Who will take care of the presentation of what? What performance targets will be set for the presentation of information? How will you ensure that management will be strong, visionary and united in their presentation of the programme? How will you ensure that management communicates regularly even when there is no news to report? How will you ensure that the messages being sent are consistent, internally and over time?

PERFORMANCE

What targets and outcome measures will be set for the operation of the change process? The presentation? The planning? The specific people? The purpose? How will performance be assessed? What process will be used? How will performance feedback be presented?

RELATING THE 9 RS TO THE 6 PS

Expressed in full, the relationship between the 9 Rs and 6 Ps can be seen as follows. In each R, you consider how it will be achieved with each of the 6 Ps:

- **Realisation** – Purpose, Planning Presentation, Process, People, Performance
- **Rallying** – Purpose, Planning Presentation, Process, People, Performance
- **Recognition** – Purpose, Planning Presentation, Process, People, Performance
- **Reframing** – Purpose, Planning Presentation, Process, People, Performance
- **Re-visioning** – Purpose, Planning Presentation, Process, People, Performance
- **Redesigning** – Purpose, Planning Presentation, Process, People, Performance
- **Re-aligning** – Purpose, Planning Presentation, Process, People, Performance
- **Revising** – Purpose, Planning Presentation, Process, People, Performance
- **Retaining** – Purpose, Planning Presentation, Process, People, Performance

In the following three chapters, we will consider each of the 9 Rs in turn.

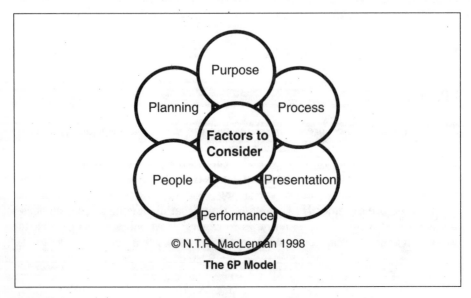

© N.T.R. MacLennan 1998

The 6P Model

11 Realisation, Rallying, Recognition

Each of the 9 Rs will be presented by starting with the objectives for that R phase, an explanation of the general principles which apply to it, followed by the key issues affecting that R. The input from the 6P Model to that R phase will then be explained, followed by an explanation of the barriers at that stage, then the issues involved in transition to the next stage.

REALISATION

The objective of this section is: to make you aware of what starts the change or alignment process.

The objectives of the Realisation phase are: to identify that there is a problem, and to define and articulate what the problem is.

The following general principles apply:

- No organisation changes unless and until someone in that organisation realises that there is a need to change.
- Realisation is useful only if the need for change can be precisely identified and articulated.
- For that to happen, someone must know the factors that force change, and at least be aware of the consequences of failure to change.

REALISATION: THE WAKE-UP CALL

Usually, the wake-up call comes in the form of losses or reduced profits, reduced market share, increased competition, a take-over bid, the retirement of the CEO and the discovery of the full picture, or all of these. 'Change is needed' signals usually have to be pretty loud before they are heeded. Usually, there is a crisis, in nearly 60 per cent of cases. Let's look at what causes change-need realisation in a bit more detail.

The wake-up call

Exercise: What was the wake-up call for your last significant change? Was it a crisis?

WHAT FORCES OR TRIGGERS CHANGE?

Two basic forces change cultures: internal and external pressures. The competitive health of an organisation is largely determined by whether it responds to change, reacts to change or fails to change; whether the change happens voluntarily or is undertaken only when there is no choice. Before we look at internal and external pressures, we should look at a pressure that falls into both categories.

Stakeholder groups

Any of the stakeholder groups can force change either actively or passively, directly or indirectly.

If your staff do not buy into your stated objectives, you will be forced to change. If your staff turnover is increasing and you can no longer keep good staff even if you can recruit them, you will be forced to change.

If your suppliers are no longer prepared to do business with you because word has got around about your payment record or your bullying of suppliers, you will be forced to change.

If your investors are making threatening noises because you are not delivering as well as other potential homes for their money, you will be forced to change.

If your customers vote with their currency and buy someone else's offerings, you will be forced to change.

If the community disapprove of your corporate behaviour, because they form all parts of the above groupings, you will be forced to change. (Even if you are right and they are wrong – remember the Shell Brent Spa fiasco with Greenpeace. Greenpeace persuaded the public that Shell were about to commit some heinous environmental catastrophy. Although Shell's record is far from pristine, on this occasion they were forced to incur huge costs to ameliorate a hostile stakeholder group which was acting on incorrect information.)

Exercise: What stakeholders' pressures to change are currently being experienced by your organisation, and from what specific sources?

EXTERNAL FACTORS FORCING CHANGE

Many factors beyond your control, and even beyond your influence, can and do cause or even force change. Here are some of the most powerful:

- technological or methodological advances (currently most notably IT advances)
- globalisation – and the consequent dropping of labour rates
- freeing up of markets world-wide
- business transfer (bought or sold)
- bureaucratic and tax burden changes
- increased outsourcing of non-core activities
- increased democratisation of the workplace

There are many others, most of which fall into the above categories, only a few of which you may have some influence on.

HANDLING EXTERNAL CHANGE

However external change is imposed on organisations – whether by government, by technology or, more usually, by competition – it can be responded to in many

169

ways: quickly, slowly, completely, partially, one bit at time or all at once. Change can be forced or voluntary.

More important than what powerful force initiates change is the way your organisation responds to it.

Exercise: What external forces to change are working on your organisation now, and how powerful is each?

INTERNAL CHANGE

Internal change (forced or voluntary) can be brought about by a strong leader or leading group, or through some innovation or invention (process or product). Of the latter two, if they are to be accepted and disseminated, they must take place in a culture which is close to the proposed change. The clearer the benefits, the less debatable the benefits and the closer to the status quo the changes are, the more likely they are to be accepted in any culture. The most change-embracing, innovative cultures will accept advances and changes that are more distant from their current positions than moribund cultures.

Exercise: Taking your most recent changes, how close were they to your existing culture?

COMPANY RESPONSES TO DRIVERS OF CHANGE

We have looked at the symptoms which alert organisations to the need for change, the factors that can cause change and the need for it. Let us now look at the relationship between forced, voluntary, internal and external change. As you might imagine, companies which are change-friendly fare differently in the longevity stakes than those which are not. What is the prognosis for companies forced to change, compared to those which voluntarily change internally, externally or both? The table below showing prognoses of companies in the changing environment gives some answers.

Prognoses of companies in the changing environment

	Response to External Change Pressures	Response to Internal Change Pressures	Response to Both Internal & External Change Pressures
Prognosis if Change is Forced	Intensive Care Case	Serious Injury	Corporate Corpse
Prognosis if Change is Voluntary	Extremely Healthy	Very Healthy	Athletic Industry-leader

REALISATION IS USUALLY FORCED

Organisations which realise the need for change only when it is forced upon them have as clear a signal as is possible that they are not in touch with the environment in which they compete. Changing only when forced to positions you a long, long way behind those organisations which change voluntarily because they can see some advantage in doing so quickly. It positions you an inconceivable distance behind a company that initiates or creates change.

Exercise: Think about changes which your organisation has undergone recently. Where do they place your organisation on the matrix in the table of prognoses above?

Exercise: Again thinking of the most recent changes, is your culture more responsive to internal or external changes?

Change-need antennae

CHANGE-NEED ANTENNAE

I hope you agree that it is essential to your organisation's survival that it keeps an eye on the changes taking place in the commercial environment. The need for drastic changes most often happens because the 'change-need antennae' were not in place or not working in your organisation at a critical time (if they

171

ever were). Even when change is externally forced, it only gets to the point of being future-threatening if it is not responded to quickly.

Change-initiating companies have a much better prognosis than change-forced companies. Do you consider your company to be a change-initiator? If you do, you probably have a coherent system to manage the flow of ideas in the same way that you manage cash flow. Do you have such a system?

Exercise: Does your system meet the benchmarks laid out in the revised edition of *Opportunity Spotting* (MacLennan 1998)?

Change-initiating companies are continually in a state of dynamic flux. They are continually at the cutting edge of their field. Perhaps you consider that your organisation is a change-responsive company. If you do, is there a role in your organisation which reflects that? Whose job is it to systematically examine and report changes in the commercial environment? If the answer is 'no one', what does that tell you about where your company sits in the classification above? (We take this classification to a more precise level on page 185.)

IDEAL TIMINGS FOR CHANGE

The positive way to view the discovery that you are in a change-forced company is to focus on the opportunity that a forced change presents. But what kinds of factors force change? When do forced-change opportunities arise? During a crisis: a near bankruptcy situation; emergence of a new competitor; emergence of a superior product/service; emergence of superior operating practices; any other threat to the future of the company. Such threats or crises give you licence to change in a way that would not be possible if everything was OK.

In each of the 9 Rs we will look at a few of the 6P issues you will have to consider. (The coverage of the 6 Ps is for prompting purposes only, and will appear under the heading '6Ps'.)

6Ps

1. **Purpose** – To monitor the commercial environment and the other factors which may trigger a need for change.
2. **Planning** – Allocate someone to plan such an activity.
3. **Presentation** – How should the information gathered be presented, and to whom?
4. **Process** – What should be the process for gathering the information and disseminating it?
5. **People** – Who should carry out this process?
6. **Performance** – What objectives will you set for this process, and what outcome measures will you establish in order to determine whether it is delivering successfully?

For each of the 9 Rs I will list just some of the barriers you should expect to encounter in your attempts to complete the stage.

BARRIERS AND DIFFICULTIES AT THIS STAGE

- No one in the organisation is sufficiently market- or commercial environment-aware to realise the need for change.
- Those who previously realised the need for change were shot, as messengers of bad news in rigid cultures.
- No one is prepared to be the next shot messenger.
- No one in the company cares enough about it or its future to bother reporting their observations.
- Staff are discouraged from thinking – that, they are told, is the job of management.

At each stage we will consider what is necessary for the change sequence to proceed to the next stage.

TRANSITION TO THE NEXT STAGE

Realisers will only seek to rally others behind the realisation if it is in their best interest to do so.

RALLYING

The objective of this section is: to make you aware of the need to communicate the realisation, and of the need to gather support for the realisation for change.

The objective of the Rallying phase is: to gather support for the realisation that there is a problem from those in a position to communicate more widely.

GENERAL PRINCIPLES

- Support for the realisation of the need for change is required before the organisation can even begin to contemplate change.
- The realisers must have sufficient influence to be taken seriously, and must have sufficiently powerful communication skills to convey the message properly.
- The realiser must rally the initial support.

Somehow, someone in the organisation at a sufficiently senior level has realised that there is a need for change. But unless that someone can propagate the realisation, nothing will happen. There is a clear need for the realiser(s) of the need for change to make others aware of that need. In most successful change situations, a small but powerful group of people rally together to start raising the organisation's awareness of the need for change. Until that happens,

173

change is not possible. Rallying can take a very, very long time: years, even decades.

Exercise: Thinking of your last change initiative, how long did it take the ralliers to get support?

DEAD MESSENGER SYNDROME

If you are amongst the people who first realise that there is a problem, only one thing matters: communication. You must get the message out. Yes, you will be at risk of being the messenger who gets shot. Most bearers of bad news in badly managed companies do get blamed for the bad news. If you are more interested in protecting your career than doing what is right for your company, then sit on your hands. Don't worry, you won't be alone. Millions do that all over the world every day. If you are happy with that, you just carry on. But those destined to rise to positions of leadership have this really strange notion: to become a top leader you must show top leadership. That means showing the way. That means charting the rocky coastline and plotting a course to ensure that the ship is not wrecked on it.

Exercise: How will you resolve the conflict between aspiring to top leadership and aspiring to avoid being the next victim of dead messenger syndrome?

I'm in no position to rally support or change anything.

Yes, you are! You can see the need for change, and you are in a position to use the fact that you care to seek to persuade those who can do something about it. As long as you are constructively critical and genuinely care about the future of the organisation, and are persistent, your realisation will be heard. If you do suffer a nasty bout of dead messenger syndrome, wouldn't you be better off in an organisation that values your concern for its future?

COMMUNICATION

In failed-change situations, something quite different happens. Most companies have seen failed change initiatives, so you can probably draw on your own experience here. You have probably seen many situations in which one or a few people have tried to rally others to the realisation that change is needed. Even when the realisers are right, they often fail. Why? Because they fail to communicate the message widely enough. The reasons why that may happen are given in the barriers section (see pages 133–161).

The main point is: if the realisers of the need to change do not rally support, for whatever reason, nothing will happen. Well, nothing positive will happen. A lot of negatives will happen: the organisation will continue as it is and grow

Dead messenger syndrome

increasingly distant from its commercial environment, and increasingly vulnerable to collapse.

Exercise: Carry out some research into company failures. Find out how long a company can get away with being out of touch with its marketplaces – 'marketplaces' (plural) because all companies have several markets: customers, staff, investors, suppliers, the community, regulatory authorities . . .

6Ps

1. **Purpose** – To gather together enough people who realise that there is a problem to influence others to arrive at a similar awareness.
2. **Planning** – The first few realisers plan to raise the awareness of others in the company.
3. **Presentation** – How is the information about the perceived problem to be presented so that it is sufficiently serious to raise awareness without being 'over-presented' to the point where it is not taken seriously? Even where the

175

problem is genuinely extremely serious, it may be thought to be hype on the part of the presenters.

4. **Process** – What process will the realisers use to convey the information about the problem?
5. **People** – The realisers decide who to approach in order to raise awareness. If you are a realiser, who should that be?
6. **Performance** – Is the performance of the realisers such that they will be credible sources of information about an organisation problem? Many an organisational disaster has been foreseen yet allowed to happen because the person foreseeing it has been too junior to be taken seriously. (The NASA *Challenger* disaster is a case in point. A junior engineer reported that the fuel o-rings would fail, and was ignored. They failed.)

BARRIERS AND DIFFICULTIES AT THIS STAGE

- The realiser is too junior to be taken seriously.
- The realiser is politically tainted, so cannot rally support, despite being 100 per cent right.
- Executions of previous messengers may not deter the realiser, but it may keep the lips of the potential ralliers tightly shut.
- Too few people have realised the need for change.
- Too few senior people have realised the need for change.
- The realiser's communication skills are not up to the job.
- The ralliers' communication skills are not up to the job.

TRANSITION TO THE NEXT STAGE

The ralliers must be of sufficient seniority, sufficient in number and sufficiently good communicators to enable transition to the next stage.

RECOGNITION

The objective of this section is: to make you aware of what it takes to get recognition of the need to change/align.

The objectives of the Recognition phase are: to recognise in full that there is a problem; to get to the point where enough people acknowledge that there is a problem, and the need to solve it, that doing so becomes a realistic possibility.

GENERAL PRINCIPLES

- A sufficient number of people in the organisation must recognise the need for change before there is any chance of success.
- Since the top team control the allocation of resources, they must be totally behind the need for change if anything is to happen.

Critical mass

CRITICAL MASS

Note that realisation is quite different from recognition. Realisation is about someone becoming aware of the problem; rallying is about that person getting others to share that realisation; recognition, for a company, can be deemed to have occurred upon reaching the point of critical mass of people who are aware of the problem *and* acknowledging that something needs to be done about it.

If change is to be effective, it must involve as many people in the organisation as possible, and that means recruiting them to help with a particular phase; that means communicating the details of the particular phase to as many people as possible. If people do not recognise the need for change, they will not co-operate with attempts to change.

The exact size of critical mass varies between company culture, industry type, leadership strength, and so on. The point is, until you reach that critical mass and people recognise that something needs to be done about the problem, nothing will happen.

Most organisations grossly underestimate just how much communication is required to get to the point of critical mass. Many even try to effect change before they have communicated the need for it. You can imagine, or maybe have witnessed, how unsuccessful that is likely to be. By creating the recognition for change, you trigger the desire for change. No desire, no change. No change, no company.

Exercise: Thinking of the most recently failed change attempts in your company, how much of your internal communication was dedicated to the process? Are the measures of internal communication effectiveness even in place to enable you to answer that question?

RECOGNISING WHAT THE PROBLEM IS

If a formal team has not been put together to respond to the ralliers' concerns, change-recognition is often triggered by an informal team made up of the original ralliers and a few others. By this time they are aware that they need to learn as much as possible about the problem and how to communicate it effectively.

That is one scenario: the volition scenario. More usually what happens (in the first three of the 9R stages) is that once a few people have realised that there is a problem, they report it to the highest levels. It is then normally denied or ignored for some considerable time until a sufficient number of people have rallied together and start making louder noises than the initial few were capable of. Then, and usually only then, the company starts to recognise that there is a problem.

THE FIRST SERIOUS RESISTANCE TO CHANGE

During recognition, emotional reactions surface which are strong and varied. Recognition by some usually triggers denial, resistance, conflict, delight, relief and many other emotions in others. Those frustrated by the status quo are delighted that at last senior management have taken off their blindfolds. Those happy with the status quo go through the classic grief cycle.

When change has become a central part of a culture, the strong emotional reactions associated with recognition are rarely seen. Change has itself become just another business process with which to get the job done.

GRIEF CYCLE

Here is the cycle of emotional and mental states people go through when confronted with some loss or setback:

1. Denial
2. Depression
3. Acceptance
4. Recovery
5. Post-recovery

When faced with the death of a close relative, most people go into denial. They refuse to accept that it has happened. After some time the evidence becomes overwhelming, and the denial changes into depression.

That is the situation when the evidence is overwhelming. Can you imagine how long and strong the denial period can be when there is no such overwhelming evidence? You don't have to imagine. Just remember that last failed change initiative. Think of those people who (overtly or covertly) refused to co-operate with the programme on the grounds that 'There is no need for change.' Even rational, intelligent, well-educated people will go into denial if the loss to them indicated or implied by the 'alleged problem' is anything other than trivial. In this instance, 'loss' can mean simply changing a well-ordered and comfortable routine, or being faced with a situation in which they will not know the rules of the new game if they allow the game to change. (Much more information on the grief cycle is available in *Counselling for Managers*, MacLennan 1996.)

6Ps

1. **Purpose** – To get as many people in the company as possible to recognise that there is a problem, the nature of the problem, and that something needs to be done about it.
2. **Planning** – Plan how to achieve the widespread recognition.
3. **Presentation** – How will the communication about the problem be achieved? How will it be presented to the various groupings in the organisation?
4. **Process** – What form will the communication about the problem take, and what process will be used to achieve it?
5. **People** – Who will it be aimed at? Who will conduct the communication?
6. **Performance** – What objectives will be set, and what outcome measures will be used to assess when you have reached the critical mass of recognition?

BARRIERS AND DIFFICULTIES AT THIS STAGE

- grief (see page 178)
- complacency (see page 157)
- denial (see page 137)
- minimal return (see page 142)
- initiative fatigue (see page 148)

TRANSITION TO THE NEXT STAGE

Only when you have reached critical mass is it worth trying to reframe or redefine the need for change. If reframing is not necessary (it usually is), you may be able to skip to the Re-visioning stage.

12 Reframing, Re-visioning, Redesigning

REFRAMING

The objective of this section is: to make you aware that the need for change, as defined by those who recognise the need, is probably not the real need.

The objective of the Reframing phase is: to redefine the problem in a way that takes self-reponsibility and is in line with commercial reality.

GENERAL PRINCIPLES

- Companies rarely define their problems in terms of their own behaviour.
- Until a company defines its problems in terms that it can take responsibility for, there is no hope of successful change or alignment.
- To reframe, you must know what you are dealing with in reality, not just in theory.

WHAT IS REFRAMING?

Reframing (or if you prefer, redefining) is about getting those involved to see the effects their perceptions about the problem have on the problem. It is about getting them to see how their current perceptions will make a solution imposs- ible, and showing them some alternative interpretations. The way the company defines the problem may make it impossible to solve.

Reframing is not always necessary. If the main group involved in realising that there is a problem have fully recognised the need for change, no reframing is necessary. But if you are in a situation where only a few have fully recognised the need for change, the remainder of the main group are still perceiving the situation through their previous awareness.

HOW CAN YOU TELL IF REFRAMING IS NECESSARY?

It is necessary if the company recognises that it has a problem, but it cannot or will not see any workable solutions, or if its proposed solutions are calls to change things beyond your control. 'Cannot see' may be caused by simply thinking in a way that makes the problem impossible to comprehend. 'Will not see' may be caused by holding some cherished belief which is seriously threatened by the problem.

Reframing

HANDLING THE REFRAMING

Reframing is best conducted by comparing the perceptions of the situation with the real, hard evidence about the situation. Here are some examples:

> Many people are saying that things are getting better, but the organisation is losing 2 per cent of its customers per year. Can you explain that to me?

> Some people have said that the competition is no threat, but they are mopping up

181

virtually all of the new customers entering the market. What is so attractive in the competitor's offering?

The threat is perceived to be 'out there', in the environment, but our competitor is operating in exactly the same commercial environment as this company. How can it be that they can provide deliverables that are superior in the customers' eyes in exactly the same commercial environment?

When you tally up the number of misperceptions, you will notice a large number of them are internal inconsistencies – people hold views in one context of company operations which directly contradict views they hold in other contexts. It is usually best to ignore the minor inconsistencies between reality and perception. Stick to the main misperceptions. Stick to that which you can evidence. Stick to that which, if changed, could bring some positive results.

As we have already noted, many people go into denial when faced with too overwhelming a problem, particularly if they feel it is they who are the cause of the problem. If that is the case, help those involved to realise that anyone with those perceptions would have a problem, and that if they can look at the situation slightly differently, they will be able to see some solutions.

In many companies, debating skills are highly valued. The ability to argue that black is white is useful in public relations terms, but not terribly effective when it comes to getting results in situations in which black is black and no amount of arguing will change that. If you come up against any such people in your reframing, ignore the advice I offered earlier, to stick to the main reframing issues. In this case, present one or more of the minor misperceptions first, and let those who wish to argue that 'yes' means 'no' blow themselves out. Once you are fairly sure that they have satisfied themselves in having won their quota of arguments for the day, get down to the serious business of reframing the main misperceptions.

COMMON REFRAMINGS

What kinds of reframing might you have to do? Here are a few classics. You can often find a 'marketing problem' is a 'the market does not want it' problem; or a 'cash flow problem' is an 'our internal bureacracy is strangling us' problem; or 'an outdated structure problem' is really an 'obsessive-compulsive culture' problem; or 'an emerging competitor problem' is a 'there have been no new ideas in the company for ten years' problem. In the majority of cases, you will find that the problem that many people in the company think they have is not the problem they actually have. The problem is assumed to be out there, caused by them. Rarely is it in here, caused by us.

Exercise: In your last three major changes, how was the problem initially defined? Is there any pattern there? Does your culture habitually attribute a particular cause to all problems?

182

WHAT IS MOST COMMONLY THE PROBLEM?

Almost always it boils down to culture. Specifically, it boils down to culture standing between the customer and what the company is theoretically capable of providing. The problem can be further specified: the culture has become out of touch with the customer.

If that is the problem, then, as you might now predict, reframing is usually about getting the company managers and staff to see how their culture has made the company distant from the customer. To do that you need to be able to identify what you are dealing with *and* be able to communicate it. So let us look at that, but first we should mention the connection between change-recognition and credibility.

RECOGNISING THE NEED FOR CHANGE AND CREDIBILITY

Is the need for change or alignment caused by management failure? By failure to make the right decisions, or failure to make any decisions? Is the need for change caused by being in a declining industry? Is the action being taken in line with the mission, values and strategy of the organisation? All of the above form a negative backdrop against which you can successfully conduct changes.

If management failure to respond to change-need signals early enough is the reason that such huge change is required now, you should admit that, and put in place systems to make sure it cannot happen again, if you want to restore your credibility to the levels required to make change possible.

IDENTIFYING WHAT YOU ARE DEALING WITH

Collect and collate. You need to know as accurately as possible what is actually going on in the company. You need to know the gulf between the intended and the actual. Essentially, you should conduct an audit of the organisation's culture. No audit, no understanding. No understanding, no effective change.

Aligning a culture requires an awareness of where the culture is currently. You cannot change or align a culture in a positive way without knowing what you are dealing with. Unfortunately, many of the big consultancy firms have not realised this yet, and do untold damage to their client companies. Most start with the reframing process without first having established what they are dealing with. If you are reading this book to help you mop up the mess left by one such organisation, you will know exactly what I mean. You cannot and should not start the reframing process until you know what the old frame looks like. To reframe, you need to know how to move from the old frame to the new frame, and that is impossible until you know what the old frame looks like.

A useful tip: do not use any change organisation which does not have a systematic way of assessing your current culture. Ask about their approach. If

such an approach is not outlined in the proposal, go where you can see some evidence of competence.

Another useful tip: be very wary of the consultancy firm which provides the ideal person you want for the job at the negotiation stages, only to deliver some spotty, runny-nosed youths fresh out of school to do the job, while at the same time charging you the fees you would have been quite happy paying for the wonderful person who did the negotiations. Such behaviour is the standard operating procedure for most large consultancy firms.

So how do you assess what you are dealing with? Well, I'm afraid my best methods will be withheld to protect commercial advantage. I'm sure you would not want me to hand my methods to the above organisations free of charge! If you, as a potential client, want to find out about and use the methods, please get in touch. Here are some of the methods that I have replaced, but which are still useful.

There are no end of ways you can use to categorise cultures. Three are particularly useful at an introductory level:

- strength of identity
- adaptability
- sanity

184

They overlap to some extent, but none the less provide a practical way of processing, understanding and assessing a culture. They give you a means of recognising what you are dealing with.

Strength of identity

STRENGTH OF IDENTITY

Any organisation can be graded on the strength of identity of its culture. As you know, some cultures are very weak and difficult to identify; others are so strong that the culture blasts at you as you approach the organisation. There may be:

- no discernible culture (rare, except where there are multiple cultures for various reasons)
- no named and described culture, although it can be discerned (more common)
- a named and tangible culture, but it is never discussed or acknowledged (almost the norm)
- a named and described culture, but it is not the one which actually exists (the norm)
- a situation where the espoused culture and the one in use are identical (extremely and pricelessly rare)

185

Exercise: What is the current strength of identity of your organisation?

ADAPTABILITY

At the simplest level of adaptability, there are two types of culture: rigid and flexible. But that classification is not sufficiently informative. In education we have the 3 Rs, in classifying culture adaptability we have the 4 Rs:

1. **Rigid** – Nothing changes under any circumstances.
2. **Reactive** – Change only happens when forced, and only happens in the way it is forced.
3. **Responsive** – Change happens in response to outside influences, and the way change occurs is chosen.
4. **Recreative** – Change is initiated by this type of organisation, both internally and externally. Others are forced to change to follow their lead.

Exercise: How adaptable do you think your culture currently is?

SANITY

Mental health is the ideal analogy to describe cultures; some of the behaviour in the organisations so described would be deemed evidence of mental health problems if exhibited in individuals. Those of you disinclined to call a spade 'a non-rigid materials manual locational transfer resource' might find this classification refreshing:

1. Catatonic
2. Manic
3. Machiavellian/paranoid
4. Obsessive-compulsive
5. Normal
6. Advanced

Catatonic cultures are characterised as follows:

- Rigid behaviour only is exhibited.
- Reactive behaviour is so tightly self-controlled as to be virtually undetectable.
- Nothing is done which is not planned, authorised and checked.
- For dismissal, just add one minor breach of protocol.
- The type of people attracted to such a culture exhibit low initiative, high compliance, limited talent, little personality – in short, they could not cut it in dynamic cultures.

Machiavellian/paranoid cultures are characterised as follows:

- Personal positioning and authority are much more important than getting the job done.

186

- Customers are those inconvenient things that break up the serious business of politicking.
- They are riven with factional in-fighting, blaming and backstabbing.
- Everyone spends much time covering their back and looking over their shoulder to see which of their 'friends' is holding the knife this time.
- People who choose to enter and remain in these organisations have excellent personal presentation skills, but little concern for or ability to deliver real results. They epitomise the insult: 'the ultimate triumph of style over content'.
- Results-focused people leave such organisations as soon as they realise what they have entered.

Machiavellian cultures

The larger legal, accounting and consulting firms are widely reputed to typify this kind of culture.

Obsessive-compulsive cultures are characterised by the following:

- It is more important to wash the hands than to do anything with them when they are clean.
- Processes become more important than the outcomes they were originally set up to deliver.

Of course, process is extremely important, but in these organisations it stands between the staff and the customers. Academic institutions typify this kind of culture, but also have characteristics of the paranoid.

Manic cultures are characterised as follows:

- There is no clearly defined culture, and there are many subcultures.
- Most subcultures are at war with the others.
- Continual change is the norm, but it is so unfocused and so disorganised that it is rarely effective, lasting or permanent.

New organisations that depend on the skills of a few extremely talented people typify this culture. Good leadership can change these organisations into advanced cultures quite quickly.

Normal cultures are characterised as follows:

- There is a concern for those the organisation is in existence to serve – the customers.
- Whether in the manufacturing or service sectors, these cultures exist to please the customer.
- Staff have the authority to do whatever is necessary to achieve the agreed customer goals.
- Goals at all levels are very clearly defined.
- Shared, transparent and articulated values guide the behaviour of all in the organisation.

Successful – but not the *most* successful – companies across all sectors make up this group.

Advanced cultures are characterised as follows:

- They display all the characteristics of the normal culture.
- They are responsive to and anticipate change, and initiate change.
- Staff not only have authority to act, they are involved in decision-making.
- There should be no interference, no 'bossing'; staff are given very high degrees of autonomy.
- Staff are expected to take total responsibility for their performance, and that includes being authorised to seek help and support when required, and an obligation on each individual to make sure that their objectives are clearly set.

There is a widespread misperception that most companies with this kind of culture are only in hi-tech industries. That is not so. Advanced cultures can be found in Semco, Nike, Gore and many others, none of which are high-tech industries (their main products being pumps, sports shoes and rainwear respectively – not exactly rocket science!).

Exercise: Which category is your company closest to fitting? If none is applicable, which combination of types best matches your company?

HORROR CULTURES (THE RIGIDS)

Rigid cultures are full of arrogance, bureaucratic centralisation and self-interest. Managers in such organisations (few are prepared to acknowledge that they are) make it impossible for their subordinates to implement beneficial changes. Consequently, bright people who want to make a positive contribution to the world leave. It becomes increasingly difficult to get bright, initiative-laden people to even apply for positions in the organisation. The few who do soon pick up the signals at the interview stage. What are the signals?

- They use psychometric testing when it is abundantly clear from biographical evidence that the individual has the skills required – for instance, giving a maths graduate a numeracy test, or an English language graduate a verbal skills test.
- They have interview processes that require high degrees of compliance on the part of the interviewee. Interview situations are clearly designed to send authority signals to interviewees.

Can you imagine how it feels to work in one of those cultures? Images of Munch's *Scream* come to mind. Why do people put up with it? The answer is that talented people won't. So who *will* put up with it? Those who can go nowhere else. What does that mean? It means that those organisations are staffed by low-capability conscripts. Long-term result: an organisation full of compliant morons, and eventual collapse.

Exercise: Name five horror cultures with which you are unfortunate enough to have contact.

FROM BEAUTY TO BEAST

Even advanced companies that were once at the top of the commercial world can be brought to their knees by their increasingly rigid cultures. Why did General Motors, Sears and IBM lose it? Because they were strangled by their rigid cultures. They went from the most dominant companies on earth to also-rans because of rigid, stifling and unresponsive cultures.

PRE-CHANGE CULTURE CHANGE

Successful changes in operations, structure and strategy are more difficult in catatonic, manic, Machiavellian/paranoid and obsessive-compulsive cultures until those cultures themselves are changed towards the normal and advanced cultures.

Going back to our rigid/flexible classification, the more flexible the culture, the more it responds to the need for change, and the more it embraces change. Such organisations are those that are thriving in the fast-change environment of today.

The more rigid an organisation, the less it responds to the needs of the customer and other stakeholder groups, and the shorter will be the period before its demise.

The more rigid a culture, the more the culture itself needs to be changed before any other change is realistically achievable. Usually, change of that order requires a new CEO, a new chairperson and often an entirely new board of directors (once the first two are in place). Why? Because the incumbents have been promoted from within, and were selected for their match to the very culture which is causing the problem. They almost certainly epitomise the problematic culture, and were definitely responsible for its perpetuation.

Such mass replacement only happens when a major institutional shareholder makes it clear that re-election of directors will not be happening, or when the

190

inevitable collapse happens and other companies pick up the assets. Rarely do purchasing companies have an interest in keeping the people whose culture was responsible for the demise of the company they are buying. Would you want proven incompetents in your company?

COMBINING THE CULTURAL CLASSIFICATIONS

Earlier, we had a simple means of prognostication for companies that changed voluntarily or under force. Let's make that tool a little more sophisticated by incorporating the 4R classification and placing that alongside the sanity format (see the table below, which combines the cultural classifications: the length of 'short', 'medium' and 'long' vary from industry to industry; in the IT industry, product lifecycles are down to six to nine months at the time of writing; in the domestic furniture market, the cycles are much longer).

Combining the cultural classification

4R Classification	Sanity Classification	Cultural Adaptability to:		
		External Change Pressures	Internal Change Pressures	Both
Rigid	Catatonic Machiavellian Obsessive-compulsive	Corpse Soon	Corpse Soon	Corpse Very Soon
Reactive	Manic	Short-term Survivor	Short-term Survivor	Medium-term Survivor
Responsive	Normal	Medium-term Survivor	Medium-term Survivor	Long-term Survivor
Recreating	Advanced	Long-term Leadership	Long-term Leadership	Dominant Leadership: Very Long-term

Exercise: Given your answer to the previous exercises, where would you place your organisation in the matrix in the combined cultural classifications table above?

6Ps

1. **Purpose** – To define the problem in terms closer to commercial reality.
2. **Planning** – Plan the reframing.
3. **Presentation** – How should the clash between the current definition of the problem and the reality of the problem be presented and handled?
4. **Process** – What process will be used to confront and challenge those who hold misconceptions?
5. **People** – Who should conduct the reframing – a very senior person, or an outsider who has no axe to grind or has no political history with the organisation?

191

6. **Performance** – What objectives should you set, and what outcome measures will assess the level of achievement?

Barriers and difficulties at this stage

- Low faith in management – they have failed to acknowledge that their lack of response or inadequate responses are the reasons such drastic change is now required.
- A blame culture – 'Our problems are *their* fault.'
- Blocking redefining of the problem, because in so doing it is implied that the problems are the fault of the company (it does, and they are!).
- Blocking redefinition in terms that would imply undesired changes.
- Refusal to acknowledge the realities of the company culture; insisting that the espoused culture is the actual culture (when to all impartial outsiders it blatantly is not). This is very common.

TRANSITION TO THE NEXT STAGE

Unless and until the problem is redefined in a way that reflects the commercial reality of both what the company culture actually is and the marketplace, there is little point in proceeding.

RE-VISIONING: FINDING AN AWESOME PURPOSE

The objective of this section is: to show you where the CAM starts to shape and control the change process.

The objectives of the Re-visioning phase are: to identify an awesome purpose which will unite and align the organisation to face whatever changes it must face; to complete the CAM

GENERAL PRINCIPLES

- No awesome purpose, no change.

Reams of change plans are no substitute for one little phrase called an 'awesome purpose'. If you can't encapsulate the awesome purpose in one memorable phrase, forget it. Pack up; go home; forget about any positive change. As re-visioning starts and begins to take shape, people start to become focused; emotions are more constructive and positive. Without a clear vision or awesome purpose, any changes that do somehow occur are no more than card-shuffling.

- No completed CAM, no change.

The staff and managers of the company must complete the CAM; it cannot be imposed. To be effective, the elements of the CAM must be drawn from the

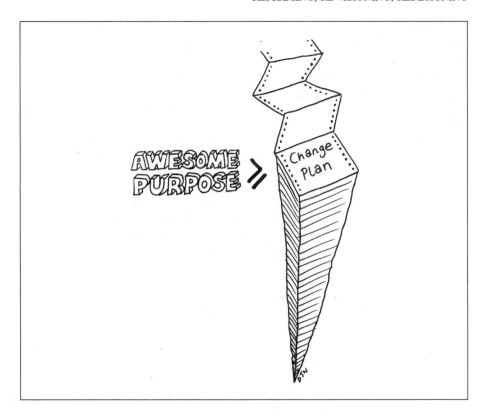

people whose good will is required to implement it. A completed CAM is required to effect successful change or alignment.

● No involvement, no change.

If they don't know how to co-operate, they can't co-operate. Visualise, articulate, document what the achievement of the awesome purpose looks like.

MOVING FROM REFRAMING TO RE-VISIONING, SUCCESSFULLY

Immediately you have recognised what the problem actually is (as opposed to the way it was originally defined) and you have discovered what the organisation culture is really like, the change solution may be incredibly obvious.

That is a dangerous state to be in. Those who understand the problem, the context and the culture in which it occurs can usually see the way forward with great clarity. The danger is that they then assume (without even realising it) that everyone else will be able and willing to follow their logic. So a plan for change is drawn up. It is distributed to those who are charged with executing it – and guess what happens? Not a lot. The plan can be perfect, but it will fail 20 times out of 10. Why? Because those expected to implement it were not involved in drawing it up. Those implementing it have not had the chance to understand the problem, the context and the culture in which it occurs. They cannot see with the same clarity that which the original planners could see. Consequently, the plan has much less meaning for them.

I know I have said this before, but it is so often overlooked that it bears repetition: those who are to implement the changes must be involved in the CAM-completion process; they must also be involved with the process of identifying what the culture actually is.

'Involved' can take on many meanings. The very least it should mean is that your people are told about the two stages of completing the CAM: finding out what the current completed CAM looks like, and completing the new CAM. In practical terms, that means at least: telling your staff and managers what information is being gathered, and why their views are sought (on each element); telling them the findings (and showing the process used to arrive at them); seeking their views on using the information to model the new CAM; seeking their views on the first draft of the new CAM.

That is the very least that should be done. Why? If culture is the set of memes shared by any group of people, then culture-formation and alignment *must* be a process of drawing from the members of that proposed culture an agreement on the memes they wish to share. In an ideal world, all of the staff should be involved in completing the CAM. Practically, however desirable, that is just too big and expensive a task for many companies. So the achievable option for them is to have all staff involved in completing the CAM at their level, as in the table below. Even that will seem way over the top for many companies, but really there is no choice. Culture alignment and change is an end which the members of that culture must buy into voluntarily. The only way that will happen is if they can have an influence.

Who completes what in the CAM

CAM Level	Completed By	What is Completed
The 'Why'	Directors	Purpose Values
Level 1	Directors	Direction Vision
	Senior Management	Mission Strategy
Level 2	Middle Management	Major Objectives Tactics
Level 3	Junior Management	Objectives Operating Principles

IF YOU MUST SEPARATE CAM PROCESSES . . .

Going back to the point made earlier about strategy naturally dropping out of the visioning process, much money is wasted in very prestigious organisations because some boffin on the top floor comes up with a 'strategic plan' that the board like. They adopt it. And it fails to deliver. It usually fails to deliver because the culture is incapable of supporting the plan. It might be a good strategy, but not for that company with that culture. Where there is an absolute link between planning the future of the organisation, managing its culture and planning the execution of the strategy (which should drop out of the visioning process), the problem of culture–strategy incompatability simply does not occur.

A culture incapable of supporting a plan

If you must continue the process of strategic planning in isolation, for whatever reason, you should introduce some process to check that the strategic plan matches the culture.

The Re-visioning stage is the one in which the CAM is completed and guides all subsequent activity. To recap on Chapters 4–7, the CAM is completed in stages:

1. Distil your purpose.
2. Establish your values.

3. Determine the direction in which you are travelling in order to pursue the purpose.
4. Pull together a long-term goal (a vision), a mid-term goal (mission) and an electrifying goal (an awesome purpose), which may be the vision or mission expressed in the terms I have laid out previously.
5. Determine the organisation's strategy.
6. Establish the major objectives.
7. Determine the tactics in order to deliver each of the major objectives.
8. Set your objectives.
9. Determine your operating principles.

6PS

1. **Purpose** – To come up with a new or modified vision that will align the company and satisfy the needs of the stakeholder groups, particularly clients and staff. That means completing the CAM (see Chapters 4–7).
2. **Planning** – The core team which has been pushing the need for recognition of the problem is normally the group which plans the completion of the CAM (or a CAM-like framework). But remember that planning how the CAM is to be completed is quite a different thing from actually completing it – that must be an organisation-wide activity.
3. **Presentation** – You must be getting bored of hearing it by now. Most companies underestimate just how much effort is required to communicate that a re-visioning is going on and that the contribution of one and all is required.
4. **Process** – For re-visioning to be successful, it must be a process that involves as many of the stakeholders as possible. How can you get your stakeholders involved? What process will make that possible?
5. **People** – As before, most companies grossly underestimate the need to recruit promoters of change. How will you go about getting people involved in completing the CAM?
6. **Performance** – Those who will be charged with the next stage (redesigning) should be those who are most involved in completing the CAM. What performance targets and outcome measures will you set for re-visioning?

VALUES, CULTURE AND LONGEVITY

Some thinkers in this field have suggested that you should identify the culture that will serve the business best, and set it up. Such advice could only come from people who have never run or set up a business or managed a culture-change programme.

If you plan to set up a culture that is right for the business today, by the time you have what you planned, you will have a culture that was right for the business of several years ago. Culture is not some throw-away thing aimed at pleasing the whims of today. It is the glue, it is the bond which transcends all other activities in any business. Culture change equips you for the business vagaries of tomorrow, and all tomorrows.

Those who advocate setting up cultures for today's business environment fail to make the distinction between values and operating principles. Hire them to help your culture-change programme at your peril!

CONFLICT OF INTEREST

Who are the people in any company who have the greatest investment in yesterday? Who are the most heavily aligned with the industry's current assumptions? Who are the people with most to lose if any major changes have to happen? The very same people who are theoretically responsible for creating the company's tomorrow. The same ones who ought to be challenging the industry's assumptions. The same people who ought to be driving change.

How many people who have been rewarded and promoted in a system are going to embrace the prospect of changing that which has been so good for them, that which they have learned to exploit so well?

BARRIERS AND DIFFICULTIES AT THIS STAGE

● insufficient understanding of the need for an awesome purpose to provide the leadership to find one
● no coherent framework around which to align or change the organisation
● insufficiently strong leadership to complete the CAM
● buy-in problems: so few people understand culture that a critical mass of people to support the CAM cannot be pulled together
● insufficient communication and education to enable people to support the CAM's completion

TRANSITION TO THE NEXT STAGE

Until and unless you have a completed CAM or some other coherent framework which includes all the elements of the CAM, you will be wasting your time moving on to the next stage.

REDESIGNING

The objective of this section is: to show you what kinds of issues to cover in the Redesigning stage of alignment or change.

The objectives of the Redesigning phase are: to design the systems and structure that will actualise the alignment created at the Re-visioning stage and which will deliver the awesome purpose.

GENERAL PRINCIPLES

Build the new design in such a way that people can see successes early and often. In other words, there must be a series of landmarks along the journey that your people can use to signal their ongoing success.

The redesign must be perfectly in tune with the culture, the vision and the market.

Redesigning is the last conceptual stage in managing change.

TYPES OF REDESIGN

We have seen what triggers change; we have looked at the kinds of cultures needing change, the timing of change, and so on. What types of change usually emerge after the wake-up call has been heeded?

- operational (technology, methodology)
- structural (staff)
- strategic (market)
- core (cultural)
- complete

THE CAM MAKES CHANGE EASIER

Today, as you read this, there are thousands of companies seeking to redesign themselves without having set out a vision for the future. If you don't know where you want to go, how on earth can you possibly design an organisation to get there? If you have not agreed what the company's purpose is and what its values are, how can you possibly judge how to redesign structures and systems. It's like an engineer choosing the tools to do a job before s/he knows what the job is going to be. Would you hire a builder to build a house without giving them a picture of the final article as drawn by an architect? Would you commission the architect if you had not told them what the house must be, do and have? Of course not. So why, oh why do so many companies seek to re-engineer, restructure and redesign themselves without spelling out and agreeing a clear vision, without completing a coherent framework within which to conduct all the subordinate changes?

Most significant change in any culture, no matter how well aligned, will cause some disagreement and resentment. The more aligned the culture and the better the match between culture and strategy, the less disagreement there will be. The 'right answer' will be very obvious from the guidelines, the values and the awesome purpose which the completed CAM provides. Let's look at the prospect of completing the above types of changes, first with the CAM in place, and then without the CAM in place.

CAM IN PLACE

Operational Change

Operational change with the CAM in place is straightforward. The culture is established, known and shared. Awesome purpose is felt throughout the organisation. Strategy is in place, major objectives, tactics and objectives are known by all. If the way those things are delivered is going to have to be changed, the operating principles must be changed. This is probably the easiest form of change.

Structural change

Structural change normally includes operational change, but does not have to. There must be some very strong and measurable benefit from conducting such a change in order to justify it. If such a benefit is there, and is in line with the culture, your people can conduct the changes within the framework.

Here is an interesting question. Which comes first, the culture or the structure? Structure is a manifestation of culture; but structure can also impose culture. As Winston Churchill said: 'First you shape your environment, then your environment shapes you.' They are interdependent.

How many organisations do you know where the documented structure reflects actual structure? Structures are usually established to formalise that which is already happening (except in greenfield sites). Formal structures almost always lag behind informal structures. Today's actual informal structure will be pretty close to tomorrow's documented and formal structure.

What do you do if the formal and informal structures are very different from each other when you are just about to launch a culture-change programme? Do you document the actual structure before starting? No. That would just add to the confusion. Let culture lead structure. Once the new culture is in place, you will (depending on what changes you are making and why) want a new structure. Most structures are entirely obvious from the values and awesome purpose. If the higher elements in the CAM are sufficiently well defined, you will find the structure jumps out at you.

Strategic change

The market no longer wants what you provide in the way you provide it, or someone else now provides it better than you do. Strategic change usually also includes structural and operational change. Only the higher levels of the CAM model will remain unaffected: vision, direction, values, and so on. Strategic change almost always means changes in the lower elements of the CAM. The higher levels of the CAM are still in place to guide you and your staff.

Core change

This requires change of the higher levels in the CAM: vision and mission. Then all subordinate levels are changed in line. Such change is what most people contemplate when they think of a major change project. With a CAM completed and in place, you have the reference point of your shared values and purpose to use as a datum.

Complete change

In companies with a strong CAM in place, complete change is virtually never necessary. Indeed, sticking to the values and purpose while changing virtually everything else is one thing that saved IBM in its recent crisis. If complete change is required, you should not attempt to change everything at once. You must leave something in place to use as your reference point.

CAM NOT IN PLACE

Operational Change

The further down the CAM sequence you go before finding CAM elements not successfully implemented, the easier you will find it to rectify that situation. The lower in the CAM a missing element is, the easier it is to complete the element or effect change at that level. For instance, if you have not agreed or articulated values and have no discernible purpose, you will find all change extremely difficult. Proposed changes higher up the CAM will be the most difficult of all. If there is no vision and a botched mission compounded by an unclear strategy, most changes will be difficult. Why? Because people have no framework, no means of guiding their change efforts, no way of knowing what the new game will be. It is difficult to start changing operating principles if no one in the company knows what they are, or indeed that they had any.

Structural change

Structural change is even more difficult than operational change, for the same reasons. The difference is that lines of authority are going to be changed, petty fiefdoms are going to be broken up or rearranged, and all of this is taking place on a quicksand stage with continually changing backdrops. With no coherent cultural framework, there is no anchor-point for change.

201

Strategic change

Strangely, although this change is higher up the CAM and should (if the trend established applied) be more difficult to effect, it can actually be easier than the previous two changes. If the strategic change proposed provides clarity where previously there was little, it provides some kind of context in place of the CAM. It can make changes at the lower levels possible. Structural and operational changes make sense to staff, where previously they did not. However, in companies where one poorly thought-out, badly defined strategy is being replaced with another, the change will be horrendously difficult. Add to that nightmare recipe the absence of clear values, purpose, vision or mission and you are only one step away from corporate hell.

Core and complete change

Core and complete change are simply not worth contemplating without the CAM, or at least some kind of coherent framework in place. Attempting changes of that kind under those circumstances *is* corporate hell. Your chances of success are as great as our developing light-speed travel by 1998: zero.

Exercise: Thinking of the last few change attempts, how do they fit into the picture just painted? What types of changes were being attempted? Were they attempts to change without an appropriate framework?

SOME CAUTIONS TO BEAR IN MIND

First and foremost, make sure your customer service and operations can continue to deliver as the changes are occurring. If you don't, you won't have a business to change! The organisation is there to serve the business (can you see the distinction?), and the business is there to serve the customer. So change in the organisation must be carried out with the customer in mind. No customer, no business. No business, no organisation. No organisation, no culture.

Exercise: What are the three most important things in effecting change? (Clue: the first one is communication.)

PROCESS MAPS

To engineer successful change, you will almost certainly find yourself with new processes for a large number of the deliverables in the organisation. Obviously, you as leader understand the processes of your business, but it is much more important that the people running and working in those processes know them. The better your people know the process maps, the better they can solve any problem for the customer's benefit, whether that customer be internal or external.

REDESIGNING REWARD SYSTEMS

One process that you as leader should definitely know better than anyone else is the one which rewards people for behaving in ways that are compatible with the values; which rewards staff for behaving in ways that help to move towards achieving the awesome purpose. The reward process is the one process you can use to create and shape all others.

One of the biggest predictors of success is how the reward structure in the organisation is set up to encourage the spread and adoption of the new culture. Will people be promoted for working well with the new culture? Praise and recognise those who have taken decisions and done things in line with the

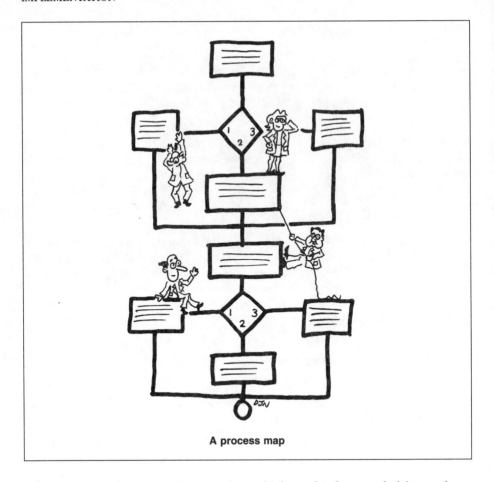

A process map

values. Will people now see the pay rises which used to be awarded for perform-ance measured under the old culture as being dependent on performance benchmark measures set up under the new culture? Make it so. Are staff seeing that recruitment decisions are being made on the basis of competence and compatibility with the new culture? Make them so. Are staff observing decisions being made which are entirely in tune with the new culture? Make sure they are. In short, are staff seeing every system, every structure, every management decision and behaviour as compatible with the new espoused culture? If not, please expect your culture-change efforts to fail.

To make the key point once more: your culture change/alignment/creation will be most likely to succeed if people are rewarded for behaving and contribu-ting in the ways of the new culture, and if all rewards linked to the previous culture are removed. (Of course, there may be an overlap.)

REWARD-SYSTEM CONFLICTS

If you leave in place the old reward system while trying to change or align your culture, you put people in the position of having to choose. The choice is between buying into the awesome purpose and doing what it takes to make it work, and looking after their self-interest. Why? They know what rewards they will get under the (old) existing system, but they don't know what rewards will be available in their changed world, or how those rewards are to be earned, or indeed whether rewards will be forthcoming at all. They will usually err on the side of not changing. Why? The rewards of the old system can still be earned: why lose the time to earn those rewards to something uncertain?

REMOVE THE UNCERTAINTY

Culture change works when people know what the new culture will look, feel and act like, and what rewards it will bring for which behaviours.

PENALTIES

You may fear losing a talented executive or staff member if you push change 'too far'. If you have decided that change is required to save the company, but you allow changes to be blocked by someone for fear of losing them, you are in effect sacrificing all to save one. If that is the way you want to run your business, you had better familiarise yourself with insolvency procedures. But if you acknowledge that no single person can be allowed to sabotage the company's future, you will want to be fair, open and accountable in the way that you deal with the human obstacles, and will wish to be seen to be so.

ULTRA-CLEAR CHANGE OBJECTIVES

Even today, the vast majority of organisations do not set clear objectives, fewer still establish clear, documented processes, and virtually none provide value guidelines. Is it any wonder that those who do so are hugely successful even though the majority of them don't do any of these things particularly well?

MAKING CHANGE EASY

If you want to make change easy, and you are not under huge pressure, change only one thing at a time. If you want to change operating principles, leave structure alone; if you want to change structure, leave strategy alone, and so on. Of course, it is rarely possible to change one thing without it having an effect on all others. But in principle, if you want to start getting an organisation used to change, isolate one thing and change it for some genuine benefit. Naturally, if you change one level in the CAM, that will have a knock-on effect at all lower levels.

After involving each level in the organisation, each level should plan the change in conjunction with those who will implement the plan. The directors should establish or re-establish the values, purpose, direction and vision, and hand their plan to the senior managers. The senior managers should then hand their finished plan to middle managers and ask them to complete their plan, who will then hand their plan to junior managers and ask them to complete their plan. Obviously, each level should present its plan to the level above, not for approval *per se*, but as a matter of communication. Approval will not be required if sufficient agreement has been reached and change objectives have been established at the discussion stage.

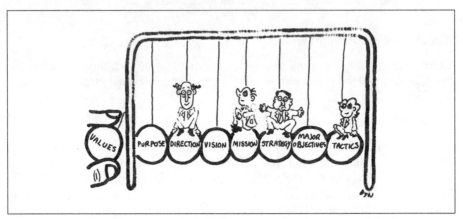

COMMON CHANGE TOOLS

Why are common tools for problem-solving and planning a good idea? So anyone anywhere in the organisation can quickly dovetail into what is going on; so they have a common language; so they can immediately know where they are in the process. Common tools and processes mean people do not have to waste time learning a whole new range of tools; they can be more productive when they move from one change team to another; they can be called into a team and be able to contribute immediately. Have we seen something like that in this book? I hope so – the CAM, the 9R Model, the 6P Model.

REDESIGNING FOR CHANGE-FRIENDLINESS

If you are going to change a culture, you might as well make it one that embraces change. Not only will it make change easier next time round, but it will make your organisation much more responsive to market, technological and all other environmentally imposed changes. The ideal is to create an organisation that embraces changes of all kinds because the constituents of its culture know that that is the best way to survive and thrive.

What objectives should you set for your culture change? That will depend on your awesome purpose, but making change a constant feature of your culture along with focused innovation experimentation would give you a substantial advantage in any marketplace.

The change initiative must be supported from the top, and the top must behave in ways in line with the new culture. Encourage the emergence of key change-managers. Encourage managers to seek challenges to their activities, decisions and so on that are considered by their staff to be inconsistent with the stated values and awesome purpose.

THE CHANGE TEAMS APPROACH

- Get small teams working on key change targets.
- Set clear objectives and performance goals.
- Set clear boundaries and parameters.
- Encourage them to communicate, communicate, communicate.
- Encourage them to share change methods and progress with other change teams.
- Have them establish a clear and common process for decision-making.
- Have them establish common tools for problem-solving and planning.

WHAT FACTORS WILL AFFECT THE REDESIGN PHASE?

- the morale of the company
- the skill and educational levels of the staff
- the level of resistance to change still present in the company
- the support offered for redesign
- the timescales set
- current work pressures
- the effectiveness of the communication
- the clarity of the redesign objectives and outcome measures

In short – the 6 Ps.

6PS

1. **Purpose** – To design the organisation in line with the culture, the CAM and the awesome purpose.
2. **Planning** – In drawing up your redesign plan, you should set objectives and prioritise them. What should those objectives be, and what is their priority?
3. **Presentation** – If staff do not know how to implement the new vision/ change in their day-to-day work, they cannot help you. You should give them guidelines. The CAM will offer those guidelines, but you must communicate that. In property, real estate agents tell us, only three things matter – location, location and location. In the alignment or change of a culture, only three things matter – communication, communication and communication. (Well, perhaps more than three, but I'm sure you take the point.)

4. **Process** – What process will you use to redesign the organisation?
5. **People** – Who is best equipped to plan each part of the redesign? The people who will be implementing it!
6. **Performance** – When performing the redesign, the presence of what factors will help you? The presence of what factors will hinder you? The absence of what factors will hinder you? The absence of what factors will help you? ('You' in this instance means you and your staff.) What outcome measures will you use to assess the redesign?

BARRIERS AND DIFFICULTIES AT THIS STAGE

- an improperly completed CAM
- an uninspiring awesome purpose
- too few people committed to the completed framework

Until this stage, change has been purely conceptual. People are now exposed to what the changes will actually mean. Visible change is always more strongly resisted than invisible change.

TRANSITION TO THE NEXT STAGE

A completed overall redesign plan which has been compiled from the plans of those who will be implementing it is required in order to move to the alignment or implementation phase. Ideally, the wider involvement of all of the staff who will implement the changes would have been obtained in the Redesigning phase.

13 Re-aligning, Revising, Retaining

RE-ALIGNING

The objective of this section is: to show you the factors to consider during the the re-alignment phase.

The objectives of the Re-aligning phase are: to implement both the re-visioning (CAM) and the redesign.

GENERAL PRINCIPLES

- This is the phase of change that tests whether all the previous stages have been successfully completed.
- Monitor the performance of the change programme, and maintain the involvement of all senior staff.
- Reward those who are achieving their objectives, and more so those who are achieving either ahead of schedule or more than expected.
- It is not completed until it is completed.

Re-alignment often fails at this stage because senior management, having done the intellectual work, assume that everything has been set in motion, and direct their attention to something else. Consequently, they fail to deliver the kind of support that staff need. Inspect that which you expect. Coach that which you hope will be completed.

In many cases, 're-alignment' will be a misnomer. Very many cultures are hopelessly out of alignment, and some have never been aligned. Just to remind you: alignment is where culture is in tune with the vision, the strategy is in tune with the vision, and all three are in tune with the interests of the stakeholder groups.

Communicating the awesome purpose and the new culture must be backed up with the conscientious removal of the barriers that stop people from implementing and achieving the changes you seek. Many difficulties will be encountered during re-alignment (implementation of the redesign). Some people may use those as an excuse to seek to abandon the changes. Removing the barriers removes some of the excuses to abandon change.

209

Removing the barriers

CREDIBILITY IN RE-ALIGNMENT

Culture is not created by memo or diktat, but by action, decision and example. Would your cost-cutting drive have any support if your chairperson was upgrading from a Jaguar to a Rolls-Royce, or would it be given a good kick-start if your CEO moved the chauffeur to a vacancy in the company and replaced the luxury car with one the same as the other senior managers? Would your employee empowerment programme get off the ground if your power-playing managers continued to keep staff in their waiting rooms before seeing them as a matter of course? Would your 'innovation experiments initiative' work if your 'one strike and you are out' policy was still in force?

Communication is understood when it comes from deeds; when it comes from words, it is often only heard. Ensure that all staff, especially senior managers, are behaving in ways congruent with the new culture.

TOTAL CONGRUENCE

To have your culture properly aligned, everything – I mean *everything* – in your culture must support your values, awesome purpose and every other level in the CAM. It must be so, it must be seen to be so, and you must be seen to be trying to make it so. So have staff anonymously rate each manager and director, including the CEO and chairperson, on whether they live up to the stated culture.

Saturation communication

SATURATION COMMUNICATION

Every internal communication must make reference to the awesome purpose. Decisions must support it and embody it. Meetings must be centred on it. Rewards must be based on furthering it. All letters, documentation, memos, notices – everything must make reference to it. You must jump on those who oppose it. If you don't, you send loud and clear signals that it is not the new orthodoxy.

211

EVERYONE HAS A ROLE

Change happens best when nearly everyone sees the benefit of it, when nearly everyone is committed to it, when nearly everyone feels that they are involved in it. Therefore, the smart thing to do is to make sure that as many people as possible are involved and contributing in the ways they are able. If everyone is doing that, hey presto – successful change. Leave people out of the change, and guess how they react? Do you want them in and doing, or out and blocking?

'EN-COURAGING' THE STAFF

Most change projects have a high chance of failure. Putting courage into your staff will be essential if you are to help them cope with the fear and anxiety of failure. En-courage them by creating an environment in which it is OK to try and to fail as long as the trying was a serious and well thought through attempt. Show them, by example, that trying new behaviours is OK. People will take the risks needed to make your culture-change programme work if they know they will be supported and guided if they get it wrong, and recognised and celebrated when they get it right.

HANDLING MISTAKES

- Accept mistakes and failures as long as the people making them were attempting to do something in line with the culture.
- Accept that good judgement comes from experience.
- Accept that experience comes from mistakes.
- Accept that mistakes come from bad judgement.
- Accept well thought through failures as an investment in the judgement of your people.
- Accept that shooting the messenger soon leaves you with no one to tell you bad news.
- Accept that listening to your staff is most important when they are bringing you bad news.

SYMBOLISE CHANGE

Think of the great plays: are they not filled with symbolic acts? Think of the greatest scenes of the greatest actors and actresses of our time: do you not see them engaged in some symbolic act? Think of the great leaders in history: do you not picture them involved in some great symbolic act? I see images of Churchill with his two-fingered V sign. I see Israeli and PLO leaders shaking hands at the White House in the USA. I see black people walking to work rather than travel on racially segregated buses. All great leaders, actors and business people recognise the communicative power of the symbolic act.

All major cultural events need a symbol, an icon or a logo. You may use a picture of a digital watch showing 01 seconds as a symbol of a 'moment of truth campaign' – one which aims to make staff aware that every interaction with the customer determines the future of the company. You may use a gleaming train to symbolise your 'No Graffiti' campaign. You may use a picture of a person on the moon to symbolise your moonshot efforts, or a person on Mars to symbolise that ambition. You may burn the company 'management bible' to symbolise a new culture of empowerment, as was the case at GE. Whatever your culture-change goals, you will increase your chances of success if you can come up with a symbol, an icon or a logo.

WHAT SHOULD BE MADE WIDELY VISIBLE OR SYMBOLISED?

The awesome purpose – come up with a symbol. If you cannot symbolise your awesome purpose, you do not have an awesome purpose.

Regularly explain the awesome purpose and its significance to everyone in the company. Demonstrate the connection between values and the awesome purpose.

Communicate the awesome purpose using the words of the awesome purpose and using the chosen symbol for the awesome purpose. This is another reason the awesome purpose must be short, simple, memorable and applicable. It is easier to symbolise single concepts.

WHAT SHOULD BE COMMUNICATED?

Ideally, *every* person in the company should be aware of every element in the CAM, and particularly knowledgeable about those elements which affect their level. In all but the optimally aligned cultures, that is not going to be achieved. So how far should you go?

The bare minimum is to have everyone know the awesome purpose and the levels of the CAM that apply to them. That obviously means there is a considerable amount of overlap. Each level in the organisation should know the parts of the levels above and below which have a bearing on their work.

Senior managers should know the elements that the directors are charged with establishing, as well as their own elements of the CAM and those of the middle managers.

The middle managers should know the CAM elements which apply to the senior managers, their own and those of the junior managers.

The junior managers should know their own and the middle managers' CAM elements.

REMINDERS

Distribute and display reminders of the key elements of the CAM. You might use things like: vision statement posters; awesome purpose statements or pictures; desk-top reminder objects; company identity card reminders; payslip reminders; report header or footer reminders; job titles drawn from the appropriate element of the CAM (for example, drawing on our fictitious instruments company: Maintenance Reduction Manager; in most companies, that job would carry the title 'Head of Design' or 'Product Development Manager' or some such, which fails to broadcast the awesome purpose).

FADING TO YELLOW

Please don't make the mistake that many companies do: to issue all the reminders and symbols and stand back as they go yellow with age. I'd hate to count the number of times I've seen that in companies who were scratching their heads trying to figure out why 'there just isn't the same buzz around here that there used to be'. If you are to keep your staff charged, you must keep refreshing them. That means mounting an advertising campaign aimed at them in the same way you mount campaigns aimed at your potential or actual customers. Do you see companies running the same media adverts for years? Not many. Most companies change their advertising regularly to keep interest in their products and services alive, fresh and current. Well-aligned companies do the same for their staff. So, no yellow or dated reminders or symbols of any kind, please.

RUMOURS 5, OFFICIAL MESSAGES 0

You know how powerful rumours are in any organisation. You know that if rumours conflict with an official message, the rumour will be believed and the official message will be dismissed as some cynical management ploy. At least, that is the case until staff see some concrete action which confirms the rumour or the official line.

In the absence of action, rumours, myths, folk tales and legends have always been more reliable than the official line. OK, so acknowledge that, live with it, accept it, use it. Do not try to fight it. How?

Communicate cultural congruence

We have already said that culture is created by, and witnessed in, each and every decision and behaviour in the organisation. Harness the rumour mill by making decisions and talking about your reasons for them. Let people know that you (collectively and singularly) chose a particular course of action because it was in line with the values. (It better had be in line with the values, or your credibility is shot!)

Make sure that all decisions are in line with the values and awesome purpose. Ensure that all communications are in line with the values. Before each decision, ask your managers to ask themselves: 'How does this decision epitomise our values?'; 'How will this decision further our awesome purpose?'

Verify that key decisions are in line with the values and contribute towards the awesome purpose. Expect that which you inspect. If staff feel that their interpretations of the values (or any level of the CAM) are not going to be inspected and verified, they will gradually move towards making decisions based on their own values as they move away from the shared values. This won't happen where you have recruited people who genuinely share the organisation's values. But since most change/alignment situations involve people who were not recruited for the values the organisation is now practising, you will have to check. Further, in organisations which have previously been poorly managed, there may be many people who are unfamiliar with the concept of making decisions based on clearly articulated values and a well-drawn vision.

KICK-START

Successful culture change is like a growing, rolling snowball: if you get some early momentum, the process becomes self-perpetuating. You need to ensure that you get some early successes in order to take the process to the critical momentum stage. You need enough weight of support to reach the critical mass that will enable the processes to continue automatically. This applies at each stage.

Success happens from that point on because everyone expects it to. They behave in ways appropriate to the new culture because they believe that the new culture will prevail, and that they will be rewarded under the new culture.

CHANGE-LEADERS

Here is a question that applies to all great leaders: how did they manage to tolerate the rise to the top in an organisation which they so clearly thought was in such a dismal state that it required wholesale re-visioning? Were they sitting on their hands waiting for their chance? Were they telling their bosses what they wanted to hear, so once 'sychophanted' to a position of authority, they could do something about the problems? Perhaps they instantaneously became inspired leaders on the day they took office? What do you think?

They knew what needed to be changed, and played the game until they could change it. What does that tell us? That there are probably hundreds of people in your organisation as we speak who are fully aware of what needs to be changed. People who could say what the problems are, but they will not stick their heads above the parapet unless it is safe to do so. If you want these change-leaders to pop their heads up, you must make it safe for them to do so. If you want to harness their desire and motivation, you have no choice but to create the environment in which they feel they can make themselves visible.

Visible change-leaders

Who are they? People who cause you problems; the difficult but constructive managers and staff, the kind of people large organisations are deeply uncomfortable with. They are critical (but constructively so); they are iconoclastic (people who don't hold the commonly shared assumptions are usually described this way – and that's exactly what you want); they think for themselves (to those in smaller and dynamic organisations – yes, this is occasionally possible in what you see as dinosaurial establishments – not all have a rota to share the one available brain cell), and they usually have a clear vision of how things should be (which, of course, does not fit the status quo).

If, by some miracle, you still have any such people in your organisation at the time when change is required, you will have no shortage of potential visions and awesome purposes to choose from. But alas, such people are rarely prepared to suffer the usual large organisation culture, and will probably have long gone. They are probably now running their own successful businesses; most people with those character traits are so disposed.

WHICH OBSTACLES TO CONFRONT FIRST?

The big ones and the ones which will stop you getting the early successes that you need in order to get the momentum going.

6PS

1. **Purpose** – To implement the CAM and the redesign of the organisation.
2. **Planning** – How will you oversee and monitor the implementation of the plan?
3. **Presentation** – How will the ongoing progress of the implementation be presented?
4. **Process** – What will be the process for ensuring the implementation of the plan/redesign?
5. **People** – Who will be implementing the plan, carrying out the re-alignment?
6. **Performance** – What objectives will you set for the re-alignment? What outcome measures will you use to determine whether it has been successful?

BARRIERS AND DIFFICULTIES AT THIS STAGE

- lack of clear objectives
- improperly completed CAM
- insufficient communication
- insufficient involvement of staff at the Redesigning and Re-visioning stages
- the realities of the change were not as comfortable to those who theoretically agreed them as the theory of the change
- a history of change failure in the company at this stage of the initiative; it becomes self-fulfilling after a while ('We always come up with great ways to improve the company, but we just can't make them stick!')

TRANSITION TO THE NEXT STAGE

All good re-alignments involve continuous revision and improvement. Transition to the next stage is required formally if the change programme has been less than fully successful, but not so unsuccessful that it has to be redesigned from scratch.

There must be enough of the plan working in order to justify seeking to revise and improve it. If it is not working, then it is back to the drawing board.

REVISING

The objective of this section is: to make you aware of the need to assess and adjust the re-alignment and the redesign to ensure successful implementation of the change.

The objectives of the Revising phase are: to monitor, assess, adjust and improve the implementation of the Redesigning and Re-aligning phases.

GENERAL PRINCIPLES

- No plan is ever perfect, and all plans have to be altered in the light of the real world.
- Set up mechanisms to collect feedback on how well the implementation of the plan is going and what problems there are.
- The entire process from realisation to re-alignment should be examined if the organisation is to learn how to make change easier in the future.

PLAN-TWEAKING

Effective change does not come from designing some perfect plan and then sitting back while others follow your instructions to the letter. Yes, I did have to say that. The number of times I've seen senior managers expecting their change plans to work unaltered is not few. Your change plan is devised using incomplete and flawed information. It will have to be modified as the flaws in it are exposed. It will be modified as feedback reveals its flawed assumptions. Plan, do, check, adjust: that is the way it should be. If you make an asinine decision (we all do and have), admit it and change it. Do not spend your valuable time and credibility trying to defend the indefensible. Do not try to cover up flaws in your plan. If you blow your credibility and trustworthiness with those who are helping you to achieve the change, you can say goodbye to it. It won't happen.

While deciding how to improve the plan, you will be faced with two types of call from your people: those seeking revision, and those seeking abandonment. In your mind, make sure you separate the two. Separate the calls for revising the implementation method from those making a play to abandon the implementation all together. Distinguish between them by the way the people behind them respond to suggestions to improve the situation. Those committed to making the changes work will examine suggestions and alter them in ways that may work for them. Those seeking to abandon the implementation will dismiss all suggestions as being unworkable or undesirable without first looking for ways to make them work.

Handling the 'abandoneers' is best done by asking them what is unacceptable about the plan or the desired change. If you can find an appropriate modification to accommodate their concerns, they can continue with their implementation. If you cannot, then maybe they have missed something in the communication about the need for change. Maybe they have not reframed the problem in soluble terms. If you have exhausted those possibilities and they still won't co-operate with the implementation, then it is time to get heavy.

Involve those who will have to enact the revised plans in the creation of those revised plans.

218

Sharing the route

Once you have found a good crossing route for one ship, you tell the others in the fleet. So it is in change-management. If you find some method of change that works in one context or location, you should communicate it to others in a similar situation for their benefit.

SIGNALS THAT CULTURE CHANGE IS WORKING

- New behaviours are witnessed.
- People are starting to openly question and even ridicule the status quo.
- Different decisions are being made.
- Customers start commenting on changes.
- Suppliers start commenting on changes.

If you want to test whether a culture change has been successful, choose to look anonymously at some small, hidden corner of the organisation. If your culture change has been successful, you will see the behavioural manifestations of your culture change even there.

PREMATURE CONGRATULATIONS

What do you think would happen if you announced that the changes had been successful before they were completed? Would that intensify determination to complete the job, or would it do exactly the opposite? What signal would such a congratulation send to those still intent on blocking the changes? 'Great. The heat is off. It's business as usual.' How are the resisters likely to behave? They will rouse everyone behind your congratulations, knowing full well that if they can get you to persuade everyone that the required changes are complete, no more attempts to change will be required and they can carry on as before.

Obviously, you must have successes to keep people going. Announce the small successes in terms of the even greater changes that are still required.

6PS

1. **Purpose** – To monitor and improve the change plan and implementation of it.
2. **Planning** – Build into your change plan (Redesigning phase) measures and landmarks to assess progress.
3. **Presentation** – Ideally, the change-promoters will present information to each other. Then the change progress will be communicated to everyone else, along with a consultation period where everyone is asked how the changes can be made even more effective.
4. **Process** – What will be your monitoring process? What will be your information-collation process? What will be your consultation process for seeking the views of others?
5. **People** – Who will collect and disseminate the change-monitoring information?
6. **Performance** – What will assist your change-monitoring and improvement efforts? What will hinder them? The absence of what will help your revising? The absence of what will hinder your revising? What performance targets and outcome measures will you set for the Revising phase?

BARRIERS AND DIFFICULTIES AT THIS STAGE

- reluctance to admit that the plan was flawed and needs adjustment
- those detrimentally affected by the proposed revision of the plan will resist it in favour of the original plan, even if that is not good for the organisation
- those failing to achieve their change objectives will resist assessment and thus revision of the plan

Some may resist revision on the false grounds that they have already successfully implemented the change. Some such resisters will be genuine; others will know full well they have not implemented the changes and will be resisting the Revising phase knowing that if they co-operate with it, their failure to change will be exposed.

TRANSITION TO THE NEXT STAGE

Once a realignment has been completed and there is no more revising to do, it is time to start work on retaining the changes and ensuring the organisation is more change-receptive next time a change is required (and that will be sooner than you and your staff hope).

RETAINING

The objective of this section is: to explain the need to keep working on cultural alignment.

The objectives of the Retaining phase are: to maintain the alignment or changes and perpetuate the change-readiness created by the successful change.

GENERAL PRINCIPLES

- Cultural alignment is not something you can do once and walk away from. It is an ongoing process, albeit not as intense in the Retaining stage as in the other 8 Rs.
- Setting up systems to make the organisation more aware of changes in the market and commercial environment is essential.
- Cultures face regular alignment crises. You should know what those are and how to deal with them.

SYSTEMS FOR RETAINING CHANGE OR ALIGNMENT

You must set up systems to ensure that the culture as it now exists is being practised consistently by the members of that culture. In other words, you need systems to ensure that people's behaviour is consistent with the culture.

You must set up systems that make change an everyday part of the culture. Maintain change-readiness and change-expectation by constantly adjusting the organisation to its commercial environment. That will make significant change, when it comes along, much easier than it would have been otherwise.

CHANGE-TOLERANCE

There is a clear link between the pace of change, the amount of change possible, and an organisation's previous history of change. Organisations with little history of change will show the greatest resistance to change. What does that tell us? If you make regular, small changes to an organisation, you can make it more ready to accept significant changes. In other words, tolerance of change is directly proportional to the amount of change. But one caution: tolerance to change can be reduced by pointless changes, or changes that have no clear benefit, or changes and the reasoning behind them which are not properly explained to staff.

Exercise: If you were to grade your organisation on its tolerance of change on a 1–10 scale from 'total moribundity' to 'perpetually in flux', what would be the grade?

KEEP THE SHIP STEAMING

The companies which achieve successful change most readily and completely are those which are already exhibiting the behaviours and habits of successful change. Companies that achieve successful change are rarely those which wish to keep a stable ship. You don't cross oceans or discover new lands if you refuse to leave port unless you can keep an even keel.

REGULAR TUNING

You don't maintain a change-momentum or change-readiness by sitting in port. Once a culture is aligned and in tune with its business environment, it is the job of the top team to keep an eye on the future and the ever-changing commercial environment, and to continue to tweak the organisation in that direction.

HOW OFTEN TO CHANGE?

Plan obsolescence. Everything that is not part of who you are (values and purpose) should be subject to a planned obsolescence policy. Every system, every process, every product, every job (not person) should have a sell-by date attached to it when first set up.

Why is that a smart thing to do? Well, do you set up a system in isolation, or do you set it up in a specific context? Do you set it up to cope with certain environmental factors? Yes, naturally. Will the environmental factors that you considered when setting up your system still be the most influential elements in six months, two years, four years? Most unlikely. So the only logical thing to do is to estimate how long each system, product and so on will be appropriate for its context, and then set a date for obsolescence.

Why? Because new competitors are surfacing every day, and they will be setting up their systems for today. If you are trying to compete against them using a system that was designed for the economic environment of a few years ago, are you going to be ahead of or behind the game? Behind, obviously. So to ensure that that does not happen, the smart option is to have in place a planned obsolescence policy. If you don't make your systems, product and so on obsolete, who will? Your competitors. The risk is that they may make *you* obsolete at the same time.

THE COMPETITOR WITHIN

There is one other group of competitors who will seek to make you obsolete – your employees. A huge percentage of the new companies set up are in the same markets as the former employers of the founding directors (about 70 per cent). What do they regularly cite as a major motivation?

> I saw a better, faster, more up-to-date or cheaper way of doing what the company was doing. I suggested it to my bosses. They ignored my advice. Indeed, they treated me like some impudent upstart. What choice did I have?

The next stage in the sequence is usually:

> Now that we have taken 25 per cent of their market share, they are starting to change their systems. But if their last redesign initiative is anything to go by, it will be just

223

over two years before they get the changes up and running, and by that time we project having taken 75 per cent of their market share. You know, I would still be there if they had listened to me . . .

OBSOLESCENCE PERIOD

Try to set your planned obsolescence period so that it is shorter than the time it takes your industry to move and change. In some sectors of the IT industry, the product shelf-life is (for many products, at the time of writing) three to six months. If you are in those sectors, your obsolescence period should be less than three months. If it is not, your competitors will make you obsolete. Do you want to control when you put your products out to graze, or would you rather the marketplace decided when to put you and your company out to graze?

DETERMINING YOUR OBSOLESCENCE PERIODS

It is not always easy to determine the period of obsolescence in an industry, but one ready reckoner is:

1. Define the parameters of your sector, and total up the number of new products per year from all players.
2. Divide that by the total number of products from the previous year. That will give you a fraction.
3. Multiply that by 12 (months). That will tell you how much short of a year the obsolescence period is.

Remember this is only a ready reckoner: this is not a book on quantitative research methods.

That may give you a false sense of comfort. Everything you decide is out of date by the time the ink dries on the plan. Your plan may still be workable, but you can be sure that it has been or will be surpassed by others by the time you successfully implement it.

The higher up the model an element is, the less frequently it should be replaced, perhaps with the exception of strategy. The competitive environment moves so quickly that good company managers are regularly seeking replacement strategies. Only when they come up with one that is better than the existing one do they make the necessary changes, at which point everything below strategy in the CAM is changed too.

So, will you be putting in place a planned obsolescence policy? If not, at least you now know what the consequences will be.

MAINTAINING CULTURE CHANGE

You have seen it a hundred times before. Some wonderful initiative is introduced into a company, works for a short while during the period of enthusiasm, and then goes sour. How do you keep a culture change in place after the buzz has passed? By putting in place reward systems that favour continued adherence to the culture.

After the buzz

MOVING OUT OF ALIGNMENT: ALIGNMENT CRISES

Companies move out of alignment on a regular basis. Alignment diffusion or focal drift occur continually unless there is some mechanism to tweak and tune the organisation from time to time.

Leadership crisis

New organisations or new divisions have an alignment crisis after the idea on which the business is based is proven to be successful and the number of people involved becomes such that a single strong leader is required.

Functional crisis

Then, when functional systems are introduced, there is another alignment crisis as the each function needs to be aligned with the overall organisation.

Command and control crisis

Yet another occurs as people start to rail against the command and control that formal structures place on them. The people who joined the company came into a fast-growing 'use your initiative' culture, and now find themselves expected to follow rules and procedures which require little or no initiative. For some, that change will be unacceptable and they will leave. For others, they will be prepared to accept the change, provided that you delegate authority to them. That delegation must take place within the framework of the CAM. Failure to provide such a framework will cause another alignment crisis.

Bureaucratic burden crisis

As the organisation continues to grow and the bureaucratic burden continues to grow, more and more co-ordination is required. At least that is the case in organisations which lack two ingredients: a coherent cultural framework, and clear systematisation of all activities. The growth of the bureaucratic burden is in direct proportion to four factors:

- the size of the organisation
- the lack of a clear culture framework
- the lack of systematisation
- the presence of management rather than leadership

People only need command and control (in the conventional sense) when the latter two factors are missing. Many companies deal with the alignment crisis which occurs from an absence of those factors by going full cycle – the business is reorganised as a series of small multi-disciplinary teams. That may be the smartest and easiest way to shake off the bureaucratic burden. But it is not without problems.

Decentralisation crisis

Where there are a large number of teams working mainly on their own, there are usually a large number of individual cultures. That creates yet another alignment crisis. Such a situation is one which conglomerates have faced for a very long time. How do they deal with it? An example replaces a thousand explanations.

ABB, the Swiss conglomerate of 1 300+ companies, has three key values:

1. People before cost
2. Think globally, act locally
3. Small and simple

Maturity and decline crisis

Here we are again, having completed the full circle. This is the point at which most cultures get the big wake-up call. The products or services in their current format have been superseded. The customers are buying from elsewhere. The company has ceased improving for quite some time. The company is aligned internally, but in all the wrong ways. The culture is totally out of alignment with its customers and most other stakeholders. Complacency, arrogance and aloofness from the customer dominate the culture. The company has become one of the rigids, one of the horror cultures. Now the sharks are circling. Take-over or bankruptcy are very real and immediate prospects for the company. Somebody in the company had better buy a copy of *Awesome Purpose* or they will all have plenty of time for a different kind of reading!

6PS

1. **Purpose** – To maintain the changes you have set in place and make the organisation more change-ready in the future.
2. **Planning** – Plan to set up systems to ensure culture-congruent behaviour, to assess the commercial environment and changes in it, to put in place changes made necessary by the information picked up from the commercial environment.
3. **Presentation** – Your entire staff must know why there will be a culture of ongoing change, and what benefits that will bring to their lives.
4. **Process** – The processes to pick up changes in the commercial environment must be clearly laid out, as should be the processes for assessing culture-congruent behaviour, and the processes for deciding what changes the change information will produce.
5. **People** – The people responsible for those activities should be clearly identified.
6. **Performance** – What objectives will you set to retain an effective and responsive culture? What outcome measures will you put in place in order to determine whether your objectives are being met?

BARRIERS AT THIS STAGE

Creeping inflexibility

Why must you work to retain an effective culture? Leaders are replaced by managers. Thinkers are replaced by automatons. 'Changers' are replaced by 'compliers'. Guidelines are replaced by rules, and worse – the policy manual! Coaching is replaced by coercion. Volunteers are replaced by 'no-choicers'. In short, there is a tendency for all organisations to move towards moribundity.

It is the CEO's job to lead the culture so that the culture leads the company. If that happens, the company will continue to be successfully aligned, both internally and externally. But as soon as 'lead' is replaced by 'manage', the rot sets in. The completion of the rest of the above sequence is just a matter of time. Warren Buffet, probably the most successful investor in history, makes his investment decisions partly on the basis of finding companies that could be run by an idiot, for nothing is surer than the fact that one day they will be.

TRANSITION TO THE NEXT STAGE

What? You might be wondering why that title is there, given that we are at the last stage of the 9R Model. There is no next stage, right? Wrong! The next stage is for your company to forget that change is necessary and continual. As sure as night follows day, every organisation, no matter how dynamic, reaches the point (for the reasons spelled out in the barriers section) where it ceases to change. Then follows a period of latency, where nothing seems to be happening, but in which the company is quietly becoming non-initiating, then unreactive, then unresponsive, and ultimately rigid. Once in that state, only a huge survival-threatening crisis will break that complacency.

At that point, the company will re-enter the first of the 9 Rs: Realisation. For most, that is too late. For most companies, their termination is self-inflicted – not by commission, but by omission.

Having covered the sequence of stages you must go through to effect successful change, in Chapter 12 we will turn our attention to pulling it all together, reaching some conclusions and presenting the cumulative benchmarks of the best alignment and change practice in the world.

14 Conclusions and benchmarks

Culture is an immensely powerful force. Those who manage organisations who also understand culture have an enormous advantage over those who do not. Those who are prepared to manage culture and let culture manage the organisation have the greatest advantage of all.

To obtain that advantage, you need to know what culture is and how it is transmitted. In Chapter 1, I presented the concept of memes. As a catch-all term, it is a great vehicle for understanding the transmission and workings of culture.

Each meme in an organisation provides guidance under particular circumstances to every member of that organisation. The management of culture is the management of the memes which members of that culture use to guide their decisions and behaviour. Its usefulness breaks down when you have to start specifying particular types of memes, mainly because of the clumsiness of attaching the label 'meme' to every item of culture transmission and reproduction. But none the less, when we talk about managing the elements of culture, we are talking about the management of the memes that make up that culture.

Understanding the relationship of each of the elements (memes) that members of a culture use to operate in that culture is central to managing that culture. The CAM laid out those relationships. If you can identify what each element is, you have the information to manage what actually is, rather than what you hope is. If you have a range of tools that enable you to identify what each element is, you can identify which of them are problematic and have to be changed.

If you have a coherent model showing you the relationships between the elements of culture, you also have a framework within which to manage culture change and alignment.

Any complex tool must be used by following a sequence of logical steps. The 9R Model specifies those steps. To successfully manage a change or alignment programme, you have to achieve the objectives specified by each of the 9 Rs. To achieve those objectives, the same issues have to be considered at each stage, and those were covered in the 6P Model. Every stage requires planning, every stage requires a process, every stage . . .

Along the way, you will encounter many obstacles. Those which are most likely to stop you were covered in the barriers sections under each P's heading.

As we travelled the above route, we stopped off occasionally to look at various models and tools which may help you run your organisation better in general terms, or may assist you with some specific aspect of your change programme. For instance, we encountered the Four-layer Strategy Model and the Strategic Monitoring and Improvement group.

All in all, I hope you will agree that you have had pretty good value for money. In fact, I think you have been charged too little for this book. Of course, as a person of honesty and integrity, you will be sending me a cheque for the amount by which you were undercharged, won't you?

Perhaps not. In which case, I ought to offer a little more.

HOW IT ALL FITS TOGETHER

HOW THE 9 RS FIT TOGETHER WITH THE 6 PS

We can express the relationship between the CAM, the 9R Model and the 6P Model as in the table opposite. Note that when the completion of the CAM takes place in the Re-visioning stage, it then influences the work in each subsequent stage. Note also that each group involved in completing the CAM does so by use of the 6 Ps, either by design or default.

BENCHMARKS

If we pull together all the best practices in all the companies examined, we can project into the future and see what the benchmarks for cultural alignment will be very soon. That is, of course, assuming that they have not come into being between the time of writing and the time of publication of this book.

In 'culture alignment benchmark' companies of the near future, most/all staff at all levels can do the following ('their' applies to the organisation):

- state the awesome purpose
- list their values
- articulate their purpose
- point to their direction
- spell out their vision
- state their mission
- specify their strategy
- list their major objectives
- specify their tactics
- itemise their objectives
- state their operating principles

230

How the 9 Rs, 6 Ps and CAM fit together

Realisation   → The 6 Ps
Rallying   → The 6 Ps
Recognition → The 6 Ps
Reframing   → The 6 Ps
Re-visioning → The 6 Ps

Note: Although the completion of the CAM can be started in the Reframing stage, it is mainly conducted during Re-visioning.

The 'Why'   Values
               Purpose

CAM LEVEL 1: DIRECTORS AND SENIOR MANAGEMENT

'What to'   Vision
and   Mission
'How to'   Strategy (Four-layer Strategy Model; SMI Group)

CAM LEVEL 2: MIDDLE MANAGEMENT

'What to'   Major Objectives
'How to'   Tactics

CAM LEVEL 3: JUNIOR MANAGEMENT AND STAFF

'What to'   Objectives
'How to'   Operating Principles

CAM → Redesigning → The 6 Ps (SMI Group)
CAM → Re-aligning   → The 6 Ps
CAM → Revising   → The 6 Ps
CAM → Retaining   → The 6 Ps

We have mentioned many companies which are very close to this level of cultural alignment, but I know of none that meet all the cumulative benchmarks drawn from the totality of best practice. If you are one such company, write to me if you want to be included in the second edition of this book. But you will probably not want to be; you will be too busy wiping the floor with the competition to worry about broadcasting how you are doing it.

In the 'second division' of culture alignment, the situation is as follows. Only a few directors/senior managers can:

- list their values
- articulate their purpose
- point to their direction
- spell out their vision
- state their mission
- specify their strategy

Only a few middle and junior managers can:

- list their major objectives
- specify their tactics
- list their objectives
- state their operating principles

Third-division companies think a mission statement is sufficient.
Armchair players are still managing by objectives.

THE CUMULATIVE BEST PRACTICE IN TERMS OF ACTION

How will those benchmarks translate into actions and behaviours? Again, pulling together all of the known best practice, the companies at the top of the food chain in the near future will be seen doing the following:

1. Company culture has been documented using some coherent framework (like the CAM).
2. It has been distributed to all in the organisation, so there is a common understanding of the shared cultural framework.
3. Everyone in the company can demonstrate that they know the culture, and make their decisions based upon it.
4. All new staff are selected for their values match.
5. All new staff are introduced to the culture in a systematic way, and know its elements before commencing work.
6. The CEO's main activity is to manage the overall culture, leaving others to manage the business.
7. Responsibility of their part of the culture is written into the objectives or job description of each manager.

8. Staff are expected to draw their managers' attention to anything those managers may be doing in breach of the agreed CAM.
9. Promotion decisions are made in line with the culture. Those chosen for promotion espouse, act in accordance with and epitomise the culture.
10. Those managers in place who do not fit the CAM or culture are given training in the company culture and how to manage it.
11. There is a continual effort to identify the gap between the culture espoused and culture in use, and to close it.
12. Cultural variations (subcultures) are encouraged where they contribute to the business vision, and discouraged when they detract from it.
13. The elements of the CAM (or whatever cultural alignment framework is in place) are continually examined for internal inconsistencies, creeping contradictions, etc.
14. Measures are in place to determine to what extent the aligned culture contributes to the business vision.

Exercise: As you probably gather, the list above is not complete. As your final exercise, go through the book and pull together all the examples of best practice in every aspect of culture alignment and change, and identify those that could be applied to your organisation.

Finally, whether your company succeeds because it has an aligned culture or fails for lack of alignment is down to you.

You have a choice: maintain your organisation as an also-ran, or unite it behind an awesome purpose and experience awesome results.

References and bibliography

Adair, J. (1983) *Effective Leadership*, Aldershot: Gower.

Ansoff, I. (1987) *Corporate Strategy*, London: Penguin Books.

Bainbridge, C. (1996) *Designing for Change*, New York: John Wiley.

Bendell, T., Boulter, L. and Kelly, J. (1993) *Benchmarking for Competitive Advantage*, London: Pitman Publishing.

Blanchard, K. and Spencer, J. (1985) *The One Minute Manager*, London: Fontana.

Crainer, S. (ed.) (1996) *Leaders on Leadership*, Corby: Institute of Management Foundation.

Davidson, M. (1995) *The Grand Strategist*, London: Macmillan.

Dawkins, R. (1982) *The Extended Phenotype*, Oxford: Oxford University Press.

Drucker, P.F. (1954) *The Practice of Management*, London: Heinemann.

Francis, D. (1994) *Step By Step Competitive Strategy*, London: Routledge.

Garfield, C. (1986) *Peak Performers*, London: Hutchinson.

Garratt, B. (1996) *The Fish Rots from the Head*, London: HarperCollins.

Helicon Publishing (1994) *The Dictionary of Ideas*, Oxford: Helicon.

Hicks, D. and Gwynne, M.A. (1994) *Cultural Anthropology*, London: Harper-Collins.

Johnson, G. and Scholes, K. (1989) *Exploring Corporate Strategy*, Hemel Hempstead: Prentice-Hall.

Katzenbach, J., et al. (1996) *Real Change Leaders*, London: Nicholas Brealey.

Le Boeuf, M. (1986) *The Greatest Management Principle in the World*, New York: Berkley Books.

MacLennan, N.T.R. (1995) *Coaching and Mentoring*, Aldershot: Gower.

MacLennan, N.T.R. (1996) *Counselling for Managers*, Aldershot: Gower.

MacLennan, N.T.R. (1998) *Opportunity Spotting: Harnessing Ideas for Business Growth* (revised edn), Aldershot: Gower.

Morehouse, L.E. (1980) *Maximum Performance*, St Albans: Granada.

Porter, M.E. (1980) *Competitive Strategy*, New York: Free Press.

Ries, A. (1997) *Focus*, London: HarperCollins.

Ries, A. and Trout, J. (1994) *The 22 Immutable Laws of Marketing*, London: HarperCollins.

234

Slatter, S. (1987) *Corporate Recovery*, London: Penguin.

Stock, G. (1993) *Metaman*, London: Bantam Press.

Thompson, J.L. (1995) *Strategy in Action*, London: Chapman and Hall.

Treacy, M. and Wiersema, F. (1995) *The Discipline of Market Leaders*, London: HarperCollins.

Van Doren, C. (1991) *A History of Knowledge*, New York: Ballantine Books.

Want, J.H. (1995) *Managing Radical Change*, New York: John Wiley.

Wheelen, T.L. and Hunger, J.H. (1992) *Strategic Management and Business Policy* (4th edn), New York: Addison Wesley.

Wille, E. and Hodgson, P. (1991) *Making Change Work*, London: Mercury.

Index

237

INDEX